# KEEPING STUDENTS SAFE EVERY DAY

# KEEPING STUDENTS SAFE EVERY DAY

## How to Prepare for and Respond to School Violence, Natural Disasters, and Other Hazards

AMY **KLINGER** | AMANDA **KLINGER**

Alexandria, Virginia USA

1703 N. Beauregard St. • Alexandria, VA 22311-1714 USA
Phone: 800-933-2723 or 703-578-9600 • Fax: 703-575-5400
Website: www.ascd.org • E-mail: member@ascd.org
Author guidelines: www.ascd.org/write

Deborah S. Delisle, *Executive Director;* Stefani Roth, *Publisher;* Genny Ostertag, *Director, Content Acquisitions;* Susan Hills, *Acquisitions Editor;* Julie Houtz, *Director, Book Editing & Production;* Liz Wegner, *Editor;* Judi Connelly, *Associate Art Director;* Donald Ely, *Senior Graphic Designer;* Mike Kalyan, *Director, Production Services;* Keith Demmons, *Production Designer;* Trinay Blake, *E-Publishing Specialist;* Sue Curran, *Production Specialist*

All web links in this book are correct as of the publication date below but may have become inactive or otherwise modified since that time. If you notice a deactivated or changed link, please e-mail books@ascd.org with the words "Link Update" in the subject line. In your message, please specify the web link, the book title, and the page number on which the link appears.

PAPERBACK ISBN: 978-1-4166-2643-5    ASCD product #119002   n8/18
PDF E-BOOK ISBN: 978-1-4166-2645-9; see Books in Print for other formats.
Quantity discounts are available: e-mail programteam@ascd.org or call 800-933-2723, ext. 5773, or 703-575-5773. For desk copies, go to www.ascd.org/deskcopy.

**Library of Congress Cataloging-in-Publication Data**

Names: Klinger, Amy. | Klinger, Amanda, author.
Title: Keeping students safe every day : how to prepare for and respond to
    school violence, natural disasters, and other hazards / Amy Klinger and
    Amanda Klinger.
Description: Alexandria, VA : ASCD, 2018. | Includes bibliographical
    references and index.
Identifiers: LCCN 2018018952 (print) | LCCN 2018019904 (ebook) | ISBN
    9781416626459 (PDF) | ISBN 9781416626435 (pbk)
Subjects: LCSH: Schools--United States--Safety measures. | School
    violence--United States--Prevention. | School crisis management--United
    States.
Classification: LCC LB2864.5 (ebook) | LCC LB2864.5 .K57 2018 (print) | DDC
    371.7/82--dc23
LC record available at https://lccn.loc.gov/2018018952

_____

27 26 25 24 23 22 21 20 19 18          1 2 3 4 5 6 7 8 9 10 11 12

# KEEPING STUDENTS SAFE EVERY DAY

# Preface

My career as an educator was fairly typical of most of us in the field—until the day it wasn't. I started out with a baptism by fire, working as the only English teacher in a small rural high school that had an abundance of poverty, awesome but underserved kids, and not much else. I loved teaching both middle school and high school, and like many of you said, "I'll never leave the classroom"—until a superintendent I admired said differently. I loved school so much that I went at night, too, getting a master's degree in curriculum and instruction and then an educational specialist degree with the accompanying superintendent's and principal's licenses.

I made the switch to the "dark side" (educational administration) when I became an elementary principal. In doing so, I dealt with the culture shock of moving from the sometimes cynical "too-cool-for-school" world of secondary students (and occasionally teachers) into the nurturing but highly excitable ranks of elementary teachers. I eventually went on to work as a secondary principal and dabbled in central office administration as well. And still, I loved every minute of it. I loved the ability to be a change agent and to work with passionate, committed professionals doing a job every day that would bring lesser folks to their knees!

My journey from educator to school safety crusader began with an argument at the dinner table. My 18-year-old son had joined our local volunteer fire department and enthusiastically taken his place among the ranks of "first responders." One night over some excellent lasagna (my signature dish), I took exception with this designation from my perspective as a career educator. "When a kid goes down in my cafeteria, *I'm* the first responder!" I argued. "I'm the one who has to deal with it and figure out what to do until *you* show up!"

Suddenly, the disparity between the skills and expertise my son had gained in only a few short months as a firefighter and medic and the complete lack of training, resources, and capabilities that I had acquired in more than 20 years of public education became shockingly clear. How was I supposed to adequately respond to the ever-increasing threats that my school faced without appropriate training or tools? On that day, I began a search for school-safety training and resources by and for educators, and guess what I found? Nothing. So like they say about changing a dirty diaper—if something stinks, change it—I got to work.

My first step was to create an organization that was dedicated to providing training *for* educators, *by* educators. After a bit of motherly guilt-tripping, I was able to convince my daughter Amanda to bring her considerable skills in technology, education, the law, and talking almost anyone into doing almost anything to the task of creating a nonprofit, education-based school safety organization, and so the Educator's School Safety Network was born. This book is a stop along our ongoing journey. I'd love for you to come along.

—Dr. Amy Klinger

I'm just helping to write this book because my mom said I had to or I would be grounded.

Seriously though, I came to the work of school safety through the side door. After graduating from law school and passing the bar, I practiced law in North Carolina. I represented criminal defendants and worked in the juvenile justice system. However, my (not entirely voluntary) work editing my mom's doctoral dissertation sparked in me an interest in school safety. Before long, I was reading everything I could about emergency response for schools, passing the time on airplane flights researching school shooters (and thereby alarming the other passengers), and speaking at conferences. Although I don't have the vast professional experience of Dr. Klinger (yes, my own mother makes me call her Dr. Klinger), I am able to bring a different perspective, helping to look at school safety as an attorney, a skeptic, a pragmatist, and a layperson. But mainly I'm just here so I don't get in trouble with my mom.

—Amanda L. Klinger, Esq.

Here are a couple of quick notes to readers from both of us before we dive in:

- Many of the ideas and issues we'll discuss in this work are better explained with the addition of specific examples and experiences. Although in most cases we will be speaking as one voice—Amanda and Amy—we also want to draw on Amy's experiences as a career educator and administrator. So as you read, when "we" becomes "I," Amy is flying solo for a bit.

- Throughout this book, we will be referencing various resources and training opportunities that are conveniently available to you in the Resources section of our website. By going to www.eschoolsafety. org/resources, you will be able to find and use the various resources we will mention along the way. Please note that this is not shameless self-promotion, but rather a response to the lack of education-specific information, research, and materials regarding crisis management and violence prevention in schools. The high-quality resources that we come across will be aggregated in the Resources section, but when we couldn't find appropriate, research-based, high-quality materials and information, we had to develop them ourselves.

# Where Did We Go Wrong?

To start the conversation about school safety, we must first confront a rather thorny question: *Why haven't we "solved" our school safety problem?* Why, as a country and a profession, is our interest in and attention to school safety only ever short-lived, reactive, and episodically focused on the most recent school tragedy?

Our experience and research indicate two contributing factors that we will discuss in this chapter: the lack of consistent information and recommendations for safety practices, and the fragmentation of information and resources between the educational and emergency response communities. We also will discuss the harsh truth that as a society we do not seem concerned enough about school safety to make it a national priority. It is our greatest hope that the loss of 17 more lives in the February 2018 Parkland, Florida, shooting will be the catalyst needed for substantive change. In addition, we will address the competing priorities and dilemmas that schools face, including academic performance versus safety (both of which are enmeshed in the need to maintain accountability and its related assets of trust and reputation), buying "stuff" instead of training people, competing interests in resource allocation, and the highly centralized structures for safety decision making that exist in school settings. Finally, we'll take a moment to discuss two concepts that contribute to the current lack of school safety preparedness: the "incredulity response" and the "normalcy bias." Throughout the chapter, an underlying theme is the moral and ethical responsibility of educators to ensure the safety of the children in their care and to give priority to safety above academics, public relations, and finances.

## How Much Do We Care About School Safety?

It seems at best out of touch and at worst deliberately provocative to say that, as a nation, we don't care about school safety. Since 1977, the Gallup Work and Education Poll has asked parents whether they fear for their child's physical safety while at school. The percentage of parents who have fears about the safety of their child's school started at 24 percent in 1977 and has subsequently ranged from a low of 15 percent in 2009 to a high of 55 percent after Columbine in 1999; as of late 2017, the number hovers at around 24 percent (Jones, 2017). School safety is, and has been, on the minds of parents.

Yet, unless an event has just recently occurred in a school, outside of the relatively small world of crusaders, consultants, and conferences, we as a society don't really care that much about school safety. Educators and administrators are overworked, underresourced, scrutinized to within an inch of their lives, and sometimes used as a political football. Should it even be a surprise that they don't have the ability to adequately prepare for events that seem unfathomable?

As a nation, we get hyperfocused on the injustices of bullying. Although bullying is definitely an important challenge for kids in schools today, a big business has grown up around it. It seems that everyone has an antibullying program that costs lots of time and money. Some parents and community members (and some educators) blame bullying for every issue a student encounters. School leaders are willing to create programs, invest funds, and allocate time, attention, and training to bullying, all in the name of convincing our students that schools are safe places to learn. Yet many of these same schools have no crisis plans or have plans that are outdated or not comprehensive (not covering all possible hazards); have not adequately trained their staff, students, or parents; and generally don't acknowledge the reality that a crisis event of some sort *will* occur. In short, despite our fears and well-intentioned efforts, schools are shockingly underprepared to face even the most common crises.

The good news is that most schools won't face a catastrophic event like the tornado that destroyed multiple schools in Joplin, Missouri, or the shooting in the library at Arapahoe High School in Centennial, Colorado. The sobering reality is that our students know when we are prepared to keep them safe and when we are not. Our youngest students regularly participate in fire drills; they learn how to exit the building to safety. But most important, they learn that we have a plan, we have the situation under control, and we are prepared to keep them safe. We often hear from parents who tell us that their children don't want to return to school after hearing about a school bomb threat or shooting. Because safety planning and crisis response have not been discussed, practiced, or demonstrated, these children do not believe that their school is safe or that their teacher has the capacity to keep them safe. How is this acceptable? Why are we as a society or as parents not more concerned about this?

## What Is the State of School Safety Today?

The section heading is a bit of a loaded question because the rate of incidents, the number of fatalities, the perceptions of staff, students, and parents about safety, and a variety of other measures can change overnight if and when the "next" Columbine, Sandy Hook, or Parkland occurs. In addition, because there is no standardized national reporting system for safety issues in schools, it is difficult to capture an accurate picture of the state of school safety. As a result, we began our own longitudinal study to try to objectively quantify the frequency, scope, nature, and severity of threats and incidents of violence in schools. Thus, we can make some general statements about past rates of violent incidents and threats in schools. According to our own research, during the 2016–2017 school year, there were more than a dozen threats of violence made against schools in the United States *every day*. As of this writing, the first half of the 2017–2018 school year saw a dramatic increase in the number of violent incidents from the year before. (Check out the most recent school year's report as well as where your state ranks in the *States of Concern* report by accessing the Resources section at www.eschoolsafety.org/resources.) Even more alarming, an actual incident of violence occurred in a school on a daily basis (Klinger & Klinger, 2017).

The 2015–2016 school year saw an unprecedented increase in school-related bomb threats both in the United States and throughout the world. As shown in Figure 1.1, the 1,267 bomb threats that occurred reflected a 106 percent increase from the same time period in the 2012–2013 school year (Klinger & Klinger, 2016).

In addition to a dramatic increase in the number of bomb threats, other concerning trends emerged in the United States related to the scope and

**FIGURE 1.1** | School-Based Bomb Incidents and Threats

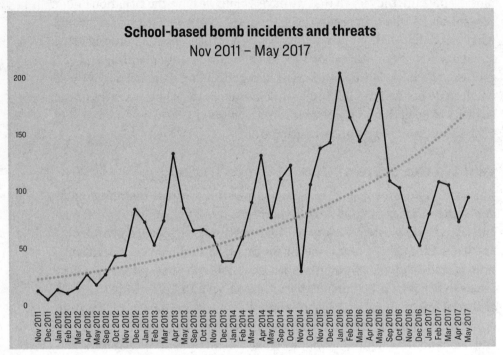

frequency of the events (more than 7,000 schools affected), the delivery methods of the threats (21 percent robocalls), the atypical locations of the incidents (44 percent at elementary schools), and the rate of actual detonations in schools (four in one year alone). For more specifics on our research into bomb threats and incidents in schools, consult the *Bomb Incidents in Schools* report listed in the Resources section of this book and available at www.eschoolsafety.org/resources.

Despite the number of threats and incidents, school administrators find themselves in the untenable position of having to make critical decisions about crisis response with few established best practices, outdated protocols, and a lack of education-based training that could help them understand the potentially catastrophic effects of a detonation and provide the requisite skills to respond appropriately and effectively to a bomb threat or incident. Based on our analysis of bomb-threat data and trends, the sobering reality is that at some point, an explosive device *will* be detonated in a U.S. school with significant consequences, and we must be ready. The question that must be considered is not *if* an explosive device will be detonated in a school, but *when*.

Although catastrophic school shootings and massacres are few and far between, the threat of such an event exists in all schools, every school day. The first critical step is to shift the thinking about school safety from an occasional concern to an everyday operation for educators that involves planning for, preventing, and responding to safety threats.

## Academics Versus Safety: Why Must We Choose?

The focus of modern public education in the United States has always alternated between "academics" and the "whole child." There has always been this push-pull between those who want strong accountability systems with a rigorous "traditional" curriculum and those who see the critical need for a school program that speaks to all aspects of a child's development. Despite the seemingly dichotomous position of these two camps, they have in common the desire for all students to achieve their fullest potential. Our hope is that this book will fulfill the promise of educating the whole child, with safety as the bedrock.

Despite Maslow's identification of safety as the most basic need after food and water (Maslow, 1943), the safety of children in school settings has traditionally taken a backseat to the primary mission of schools—to educate children. Yet this priority of academics over safety is counterproductive. Meta-analyses of research on the effect of school violence and perceptions of school safety on achievement clearly establish two important truths. The first is that when violence occurs in a school, learning stops—not exactly a groundbreaking revelation. The second, more subtle indication of the research is that when students feel that violence might occur, learning is suppressed. The mere perception of potential danger is enough to decrease academic achievement (Prevention Institute, n.d.). As then–Secretary of Education Arne Duncan put it at the 2011 National Forum for Youth Violence Prevention, "No school can be a great school unless it is a safe school."

Too often, students' perceptions of their school as an unsafe place are disregarded or minimized, primarily because perception isn't as measurable or definable a metric as "X number of violent events took place in this school." Many possible factors, such as a school demonstrating a plan for safety (or not) or how empowered (or intimidated) students feel as a result of conversations and trainings on school safety, can affect students' perceptions and beliefs about how safe a school is. In our work with schools we often talk about "unowned" areas in schools—those places where students don't feel safe or where they know violence or other misbehavior occurs. Students don't necessarily categorize these areas as "unowned" or "unsafe," but when asked where a student would go to beat someone up, smoke weed, or make out, students invariably are able to identify specific places in their school (e.g., stairwells, remote hallways, unlocked vacant areas) where they know (or at least perceive) that unsafe activities occur. When we ask administrators where the unsafe or unowned areas in their school are and they say they don't know, we tell them to ask the kids. Your students are most likely well aware of areas in your school that are unsupervised and potentially unsafe.

Many people have the misguided idea that educators should not discuss violence in schools with students because it makes the students anxious. Teachers, administrators, and boards pretend that school safety and violence prevention do not need to be discussed because violence doesn't ever happen in "our" schools. Let us assure you that students are well aware that violence occurs in U.S. schools and that bad things could happen in any school. A school's collective unwillingness to discuss that possibility doesn't alleviate anxiety. In fact, our experiences with schools and students indicate that what really makes students anxious is not that a crisis might occur, but that the adults in the school don't seem to know what to do about it!

In Amy's career as a building principal, she was always very concerned about academics, so she understands the emphasis and concern about the instructional program as justifiable and important. We are not saying that schools shouldn't be concerned about student success and mandated accountability measures like test scores. In fact, if you really want to improve your students' academic performance, improve the way you plan for, prevent, and respond to crisis events (not just violence) in your school. Show your students that their school is a safe place. More learning will take place if your students know that, if something bad does happen, there is a plan and everyone knows what to do.

## The Assets of Trust and Reputation

Current accountability and assessment systems are centered on the idea that a transparent review of a school's academic performance on standardized measures will result in improved outcomes derived from legislated incentives and sanctions as well as public pressure and competition. In other words, schools want to establish a reputation as high-performing institutions of excellence. Unfortunately, just as low test scores and high dropout rates can obscure the great improvements that are occurring in a given school, so can rumors of fights, drugs, and bullying or an ineffective response to a previous crisis event.

A few years ago, we attended a panel discussion of representatives from several Ohio institutions that had fallen victim to violence on their campuses. We were particularly moved by a marketing staff member from Kent State University. This man explained that his most important job at the university was to make sure that it was known for something other than the terrible events of May 4, 1970. In our work throughout the United States, the truth of this remark becomes so clear in our presentations. Almost everyone knows of Kent State University, but only for that single event, not for its myriad other valuable contributions to higher education. The people at Kent State get it; they understand the value of trust and reputation and continue trying to refocus the narrative.

It's frustrating to us to see the amount of time and energy that schools put into community relations—hosting innumerable breakfasts and family nights, pushing out feel-good stories on social media, holding informational meetings and parent forums—in an attempt to establish a relationship of trust and maintain a solid reputation. Yet so many overlook the most viable threat to their efforts: a lack of safety planning and preparation. Great test scores and beautiful facilities don't matter if the school is perceived as a place where harassment, drugs, and intruders run rampant. The bottom line is that while parents will forgive a dip in test scores or a lower grade, they will never forgive or forget if a traumatic event, an injury, or a death happens to their child in your school.

## Demonstrating the Value of Safety

While we're talking priorities, we can also examine the allocation of resources in schools. It's well established that what we value and find important, we spend money on. That's why people want nice houses, lots of toys for their kids on birthdays and holidays, and ridiculous sweaters for their dogs. In most schools, although there isn't an abundance of money being spent, there are fairly nice athletic facilities, decently equipped and outfitted marching bands, and relatively extensive playgrounds. An examination (American Association of School Administrators, 2010) of the operating budgets of most schools shows that 80–85 percent of the expenditures go to salaries—as it should, because education is a people business. Yet if we look at what is spent on training and professional development, the amount is very little, and what little there is typically isn't being spent on safety training.

More frustrating is the fact that when money *is* spent on safety in schools, it is most often expended on "stuff," not people, in a knee-jerk reaction to a specific event, with the goal of being able to point to the shiny metal detector or the fancy software and say to parents, "Look! Your kids are safe now!" Unfortunately, this claim is simply not true.

If the desire is to make schools safer from the myriad of natural and human-caused threats they face (not just an active shooter), then it takes a comprehensive approach in which the resources of time, money, and personnel are allocated in a strategic, ongoing fashion. Simply buying stuff or holding a "one and done" training event will contribute little if anything to progress in planning for, preventing, and responding to the many potential crisis events schools face.

In response to high-profile active shooter events in schools, such as those at Columbine, Sandy Hook, and Parkland, there has been an overemphasis on introducing full-time law enforcement into schools, usually through a school resource officer (SRO) or community police officer. Although this expensive proposition seems to solve some superficial problems and is clearly a public relations win, there is a need to critically examine the role of law enforcement in schools. This is where it gets touchy. To question the validity and value of a law enforcement officer in a school is often seen as rooted in opposing law enforcement, but this isn't the case. Educators have a professional obligation to objectively assess and evaluate every program that is implemented in schools.

We can point to many instances where the presence of a law enforcement officer in a school quite literally saved lives. That fact is a given. The resource officer on site at the 2013 Arapahoe High School shooting was a factor in shortening that event to a mere 87 seconds, although lives were still lost. We can't, however, measure the number of times the presence of a police officer was a deterrent to a violent act that never occurred as a result. We also know that well-trained school resource officers can form positive, trusting relationships with students that can help improve strained relationships between law enforcement and the communities they serve.

Conversely, we can also examine numerous instances in which officers in schools have reacted with excessive force (remember some of the shocking videos that showed up on the nightly news from schools in San Antonio, Baltimore, and Columbia, South Carolina), made errors in judgment (such as the accidental discharge in a Michigan school as the officer "showed someone" his weapon), or did not adequately anticipate the unique attributes of the educational situation they were in (exemplified by the 3rd grader who took the gun from a guard's holster in a South Carolina school).

Schools require an officer who has a foot in both worlds: law enforcement *and* education. Like teachers, an officer needs to have adequate training that is specific to education. A crisis event in a school is not the same as a crisis event in a shopping mall and cannot be treated as such. Police officers are often placed in educational settings without the benefit of understanding the different culture in which they are working. They cannot automatically overlay the same law enforcement principles and procedures used elsewhere on the school setting.

In September 2016, the U.S. Department of Education and the U.S. Department of Justice sent letters to schools discussing the role of police officers in schools and providing best-practice recommendations. According to then–Secretary of Education John B. King Jr., "School resource officers can be valuable assets in creating a positive school environment and keeping kids safe. But we must ensure that school discipline is being handled by trained educators, not by law enforcement officers." King's letter (which is available in full along with the SECURe policy rubric in the Resources section at www.eschoolsafety.org) went on to advise schools and universities to "clarify their expectations of school-based officers" (U.S. Department of Education & U.S. Department of Justice, 2016). This can be done by creating a memorandum of understanding (MOU) between local boards of education and police departments that clarifies the administrator's jurisdiction and responsibilities in day-to-day discipline, delineates the role of law enforcement officers in their interactions with students, and perhaps most important, requires education-specific training for school-based officers.

This last part is crucial and needs to be emphasized. Our nonprofit organization does a good amount of law enforcement–based training, and to be honest, initially we found it a bit daunting. We wondered, what would we as educators (albeit school safety experts) have to add to the training and experiences of law enforcement? Quite a bit, it turns out. It is interesting (and valuable) to note that almost without exception, we find law enforcement officers to be eager recipients of a school perspective. After one conference presentation, we ran into a group of New York City police officers at the "hospitality reception" (meaning the hotel bar), where they welcomed us like long-lost friends. These individuals were highly trained tactical officers as well as consummate professionals. They were also parents, grandparents, and community members who clearly saw how an understanding of the unique circumstances and constraints of schools could increase their ability to keep students safe. One officer asked us, "Why doesn't every cop have this type of training about schools?" Good question. Unfortunately, many decision makers who determine the type of training that law enforcement receives don't see this need—despite federal recommendations and established best practices. Perhaps the takeaway here is that the tools of school safety are many and diverse (from training to physical items to personnel) but can only function effectively when placed in the appropriate context.

## Decentralizing Authority

One of the most significant paradigm shifts that must occur in order to have safer schools is to move away from the current highly centralized authority for decision making and crisis response. In most schools today, we have put all of our eggs in one basket. Typically, the only individual who has had any crisis-response training and has been tasked with all decision making is the principal—the person who is most likely to be unavailable or compromised in the midst of a crisis event. Ask any principal and he or she will tell you it seems that problems occur most frequently just after the administrator has left the campus! Past incidents indicate that school administrators may well be involved in disarming the attacker (as they were in shootings at a high school in Harrisburg, South Dakota, and a middle school in Blauvelt, New York), fired upon by the shooter (as in a shooting at an elementary school in Knoxville, Tennessee), or, more chilling, one of the first fatalities, as was the case at Millard South High School in Nebraska and at Sandy Hook Elementary in Connecticut (New York Police Department Counterterrorism Bureau, 2011). When the staff is untrained and not empowered, and authority is highly centralized, the only person with authority is often unavailable to provide instructions, making the school incredibly vulnerable during a crisis event as the staff and students are left with a minimal idea of what to do or when to do it.

This misalignment is also true of most school facilities. Much of the equipment and materials needed to respond to a crisis event, such as a first aid kit, communication systems, and critical phone numbers, are all housed in the main office—the physical site most likely to be unavailable, as the majority of violent events begin within or near the main office.

Diversifying and decentralizing authority is a must for every school because, in truth, school stakeholders such as teachers and support staff are the "first" first responders. It's great when the building principal, law enforcement personnel, firefighters, and emergency medical services are trained to respond to crisis events, but it wasn't *only* those people who led kids to safety at Sandy Hook or pulled students out of the rubble of the school in Moore, Oklahoma. It was also the teachers and staff—the first line of defense. The reality of the situation is that the mostly likely responders in school crisis situations—teachers and staff—have had the least training and have the least authority to make decisions.

## Compliance Versus Engagement

It's not enough to just shift the burden of responsibility from the principal to the staff; what is required is the empowerment that comes from adequate, appropriate training. In our work, we often see overzealous administrators or local law enforcement officers decide they are going to "force" the school staff to be safe through mandated compliance. In one school, the principal stocked five-gallon buckets with a variety of household items such as tampons and bungee cords without any explanation of their purpose. Staff members were never given any training or direction as to what the items were supposed to be used for (stanching bleeding and barricading the door, respectively). Without these directives, school staff just kept this bucket of seemingly random objects around because they were told to, with no notion of the potential value.

We cringe when we see school leaders decide to "increase safety" with a series of edicts, long-winded lectures, and lengthy procedures that are required of school staff without the benefit of any explanation or training. The result? Safety and preparedness do not increase, but resentment, confusion, and fear certainly do!

Phillip Schlechty (2005), along with many others in the worlds of business and education, discusses the importance of engagement rather than compliance in motivating people to higher levels of performance. The notion of compliance versus engagement has some powerful implications not just for instructional strategies but also for safety and crisis management in schools. In Amy's 28 years in public education, there were numerous times when it was unclear why a specific procedure was in place, other than that it was supposed to be. This typically resulted in a cat-and-mouse game in which staff members only complied with safety directives when they thought someone was looking.

> I can remember being irritated at the seemingly arbitrary fire code violations pointed out by the local fire chief. Who cares if there was paper over the classroom windows? Why did it matter? It wasn't until my own son became a fireman that I learned paper over the classroom windows makes it difficult to determine if there is a fire within a given area without opening the door—which could result in a dangerous flashover.

A great example of engagement improving safety is the use of staff identification badges. We once worked with a school where staff members were told to wear their IDs but very few ever did. The principal issued memos and half-hearted reprimands telling people they had to wear their badges every day. Very few complied, and those who did were teased as being "suck-ups." This issue came up at our training, when we discussed the rationale behind wearing identification badges. We gave the teachers two compelling reasons why staff ID badges are important. First, when training students, especially elementary students, what to do in a rapid evacuation, students are often told that if they don't see their teacher, they should head for a person in an emergency responder uniform or an adult wearing a school identification badge because both would be considered safe adults. The lack of ID badges compromised the effectiveness of this critical procedure. Then we related how emergency responders often tell us that when they arrive on the scene they have difficulty determining who is in a position of authority—such as distinguishing the teachers from parents or older students. When staff members are wearing their ID badges, responders can immediately get the information and assistance they need directly from the appropriate people. After this discussion of the rationale for staff badges, several teachers turned to the principal and said, "I think we should wear our badges starting tomorrow." Because they were engaged in the discussion about the need for staff badges and understood the rationale behind them, compliance became a nonissue.

It's interesting that, in classrooms, educators take great pains to explain to students the learning objectives being pursued—in other words, what is being learned and why it is important—yet in safety training, instructors often incorporate elements from crisis-response protocols in which the rationale is not very clear, without taking the time to explain the reasoning behind it. Why are teachers supposed to close the blinds during a lockdown? Why shouldn't people evacuate to parking lots? As a result of this oversight, we demand compliance rather than engagement and are frustrated when we don't get it! Even worse, when focusing on steps to be complied with, people never learn what we are trying to accomplish and therefore are ill-equipped to make their own decisions.

## School Safety "Stuff"

Let's talk for a moment about rampant consumerism related to the work of school safety. School people, like everyone else, like to buy "stuff." The work of educating children requires consumable materials and equipment. Schools always need more calculators, crayons, and construction paper. Yet the heart of instruction is not stuff; it's content. The same is true regarding safety. Thanks to the marketing genius of a myriad of for-profit vendors, software developers, and good-hearted entrepreneurs, school decision makers concerned about safety are bombarded with apps, equipment, and systems that promise to keep kids safe. As a result, U.S. schools have spent millions of dollars on everything from metal detectors to computerized sign-in systems to bulletproof whiteboards, all of which serve only a single purpose, and they have hardly any data indicating the items' efficacy for that limited purpose. The question is, are schools really safer as a result?

We once conducted a vulnerability assessment in a district that had purchased a fancy (meaning expensive) system for each building that tracked who was entering and exiting schools by scanning a visitor's drivers license and printing out a custom badge. The first school we visited in that district was using this gadget as a very expensive coat rack and asked us to sign in using the paper "visitor's log"—except that the log was buried in a pile on a spare desk and hadn't had an entry in weeks. We ended up with no badge, no need to show ID, no scan, and free access to the building. The next school *was* using the expensive system, but our EMT/firefighter consultant (who is also Dr. Klinger's son and a smart aleck) entered his name as Daffy Duck and presented his license. The security guard conducting the sign-in never read his entry but gravely entered his license information, presenting him with a badge that had a completely different name and bore the picture of a gentleman who was 20 years older and the wrong race. Was the school safety "stuff" used? Had the "procedure" been followed? Technically, yes (somewhat). Did it help with safety? Nope.

After the tragedy at Sandy Hook Elementary, panicked school boards and administrators across the nation rushed to purchase access-control items such as buzzer systems and sally ports. The sad irony is that most of the schools purchased and installed the same type of security systems that had been easily compromised in the first minutes of the Sandy Hook shooting. Does this mean that these systems are a waste of money? It depends. Once again, the key is training. If a school installs a buzzer system but does not develop and implement protocols for its use, does not explain the rationale and procedures to those using it (parents and staff alike), and does not provide any training for those tasked with using the system to control access to the building, what has really changed? (For more information on education-based training for visitor screening, see the Resources section for this chapter at the end of the book and go to www.eschoolsafety.org/resources.) The resulting practice usually looks like this: A visitor outside the school pushes the button, someone in the office pushes a button, and the visitor enters the school without any screening or examination. How was this any different from what the school did before spending $5,000 on the buzzer?

Our nonprofit organization, the Educator's School Safety Network, is often asked to review or endorse products, software, hardware, apps, and various other gadgets related to school safety and crisis response—and we always say no. It's not that we think safety products are useless or not important; it's that education is first and foremost about people. If you don't provide appropriate ongoing training to the people who are directly affected by whatever it is you bought, no matter how good the product or service, it will not make your school safer. A tool only has utility if the people using it know what they are trying to accomplish with it. School safety stuff without knowledge is just stuff.

Another issue is the allocation of a school's limited financial resources. Every dollar that is spent on a single-use gadget or gizmo is one less dollar spent on training that will save lives. In most schools, for the cost of just a few door-blocking mechanisms or a student accountability app, schools can provide direct training to literally every staff member, student, and parent. More important, comprehensive, all-hazards training prepares people to respond to a variety of events, whereas many safety products, such as door jams or metal detectors, address only one specific type of threat.

## Everyday Safety

An important distinction needs to be made here. When school safety and crisis response are approached from a purely law enforcement perspective, educators (justifiably or not) often get the impression that school safety is yet another task assigned to them—that they are supposed to do this on top of all the other expectations that our society has for what schools should be doing. No one is saying that teachers need to go around in a state of hypervigilance, tensed and ready at any second for a catastrophic event. That is certainly not the case with our well-trained emergency responders. Police officers and firefighters do not go around in a constant state of worry about what could happen next. Instead, they have the confidence and disposition to respond that come from being adequately and appropriately trained and empowered.

The same should be true of our educators. We call this the "Project Charlie effect." In the mid '70s, schools took on substance-abuse prevention through a social skills and self-esteem program called Project Charlie that focused on resiliency and resisting peer pressure by teaching respect, honesty, and other character-building traits (McGurk & Hurry, 1995). The problem was not in the program itself, but in its often piecemeal implementation in schools. On Tuesdays a school focused on respect, while on Thursdays it focused on self-esteem. Clearly the tenets of character education are important every day of the week, yet they were not integrated as foundational principles or daily operating procedures. This compartmentalized approach is often used with school safety and crisis response. For instance, in our work with schools, we notice that school safety tends to be addressed during a professional development day before the school year starts, and then it falls off the radar. School stakeholders often go for long periods of time unconcerned with safety until a violent incident occurs somewhere, or something shows up in the media, or a minor event throws a scare into them, which tends to make them then focus too much on a specific element of school safety—like locking doors or signing in visitors—at least temporarily. The components of a safe school need to be a part of what educators do every day, coming to mind as naturally and easily as giving an assignment or talking with a student. Planning for, preventing, and responding to crisis events must become a part of an educator's daily work.

In the midst of a chaotic early September 2017 (three massive hurricanes, a heavy legislative agenda, and a threatening North Korea), Speaker of the U.S. House of Representatives Paul Ryan was famously quoted as saying that Congress should be able to "walk and chew gum at the same time" (Soergel, 2017), meaning that the government had a responsibility to both pursue its normal functions and legislative agenda *and* provide services and protection during crisis events. Although this point may be debatable in a political context, it has a valid application for schools. Is it unreasonable to expect that schools have a responsibility to educate kids *and* keep them safe? Must we always choose one or the other?

Finally, let's just lay our cards on the table. As educators, we have a moral and ethical responsibility to the children in our care. All of the factors we've discussed in this chapter are certainly important, but when you come right down to it, as educators and parents, our *most* important job is to keep our kids safe. Parents entrust to our care the beings that they love most in the world. This is a tremendous responsibility. How dare we minimize or ignore this incredibly important job by focusing on union contracts, standards, or the new science textbooks at the expense of safety? The allocation of time, money, personnel, and training for safety must come before anything else.

## "Not in My School": The Incredulity Response and the Normalcy Bias

In his book *The Survivors Club*, Ben Sherwood (2009) discusses two concepts that are dangerously prevalent in educational settings: the *incredulity response* and the *normalcy bias*. John Leach, a leading expert on survival psychology, identified and named the incredulity response after finding that people smack in the middle of a fire, a flood, or a violent event will often remain convinced that "this isn't really happening." This phenomenon is particularly dangerous because, despite the obvious threat, people refuse to acknowledge how serious the situation really is. At this point, the normalcy bias kicks in—the coping mechanism that makes you ignore that little voice in your head that is telling you to act and instead cling to the notion that everything is fine. The normalcy bias is what keeps us standing outside gawking at the approaching tornado, sitting in our seat at the conference while the fire alarm goes off, or watching the intruder walk across the playground. Amy uses these examples for a reason—because they actually happened to her; each time, she was caught up in the normalcy bias and fortunately was able to overcome it in time.

In our trainings where both law enforcement personnel and educators are present, we often point out the impact of training and perspective on the normalcy bias. We ask the teachers, "If you heard a series of bangs outside in the hallway, what would you think?" As you might guess, the typical response is to think, "What is that noise? It can't be gunshots. I wonder what is going on. We're trying to learn in here!" (And most educators would want to head out into the hallway to see who needs to be yelled at!) In contrast, law enforcement officers would easily identify those noises as gunshots, know that danger is present, and immediately use their tactical training to enact an appropriate response. It's not that law enforcement officers are smarter, better people; it's that they have been given enough of the right type of training to overcome the normalcy bias and apply their tactical skills appropriately.

A secondary issue that contributes to our normalcy bias is the erroneous perception and definition we have of a crisis event. A crisis event, broadly defined, is an event that overwhelms the available resources of the organization, requiring additional help and assistance from outside entities. In our current narrowly defined view of school crisis events, we tend to think only of (and train for) an active shooter event, excluding all the crisis events that are much more likely to occur and are equally dangerous, such as severe weather, medical emergencies, and bus accidents. We must keep in mind that any given school will experience a crisis event of some type every year. "There are two types of administrators: those who have dealt with a crisis and those who are about to" (Stephens, n.d.).

The lack of training and of conversations about safety and crisis response, and the subtle (and not so subtle) denial that (fill in the crisis event here) would never happen in our school!" make school stakeholders perilously vulnerable to deadly inactivity. As Leach puts it, "Denial and inactivity prepare people well for the roles of victim and corpse" (Sherwood, 2009, p. 37). Educators didn't join the profession to be either of these. Thus, they need to be empowered, active first responders.

# Assessing for Vulnerabilities and Threats

2

Assuming we've convinced you of the importance of school safety and you're ready to embark on a comprehensive, all-hazards approach to crisis management in schools, we'll start by transitioning from the more theoretical, ideological concerns covered in Chapter 1 to the practical application of safety concepts. This chapter begins with a macro view of potential risks inherent in school settings, followed by discussions of vulnerability assessments and threat assessments, focusing on how, when, and to what extent they should be applied and implemented.

## A Realistic Look at Risk: What Should We Be Concerned About?

If media attention, parents' fears, and the focus of administrators were accurate indicators, a school shooting would be the most likely danger a school will face. In reality, this is not the case. The myriad of vulnerabilities, hazards, and potential threats is much more diverse. It is statistically much more likely that a school will face less dramatic but equally significant crisis events such as the death of a student, a medical emergency, or a community-based disaster.

The Federal Emergency Management Agency (FEMA) defines three specific types of hazards for which schools should be prepared: human-caused hazards, natural hazards, and technological hazards. Let's look at each in turn.

*Human-caused hazards* are those that arise from either the deliberate or unintentional actions of human beings. These include violent events such as an assault or a shooting, as well as accidental incidents or injuries. In a school setting, hazards caused by humans can arise from many different factors, including a lack of violence-prevention activities, a negative school climate, inadequate supervision, or dangerous conditions in the physical plant. As anyone who has ever supervised recess can attest, sometimes, despite our best efforts, accidents are inevitable due to the sheer number of individuals who occupy a given space. It is critical to understand that although not all human-caused hazards can be prevented, the severity and impact of incidents can be mitigated with proper planning and training. The fact that some measure of risk is inevitable doesn't mean we can't work to reduce that risk and its effects.

*Natural hazards* are those that are related to weather patterns or physical conditions in the area of the school. Depending on their geographic location, nearly all schools and their surrounding communities are exposed to a variety of natural hazards or severe weather events such as floods, earthquakes, or fires. Typically, these natural hazards occur with some frequency in the given geographical area, allowing schools to give priority to planning for the most likely natural hazards.

*Technological hazards* are often overlooked but arise from technological, industrial, or infrastructure accidents or failures such as a hazardous-material incident or failures of dams, power, or telecommunications systems. Natural disasters often trigger a domino effect of multiple technological or infrastructure failures that have a significant community-wide impact, decreasing the number of resources and the amount of support that the school can access for assistance.

FEMA and the Department of Education offer many resources that can help schools assess the type of hazards they are most likely to face. See the Resources section at the end of this book for just a few.

## Vulnerability Assessments: How Do We Know What to Prepare For?

In a discussion of planning for and mitigating risks, it's important to understand the different approaches used to determine the threats a school faces. The terms *vulnerability assessment* and *threat assessment* are often used interchangeably within both the education and emergency-response worlds. Let's clarify the differences between them.

Vulnerability assessment and threat assessment are both critical components of every school's work to prevent violence in schools—the former as a regularly scheduled activity, and the latter when threats or concerns about individuals arise. The difference is in focus (see Figure 2.1). Vulnerability assessments focus on things, not people. A vulnerability assessment can be planned in advance and looks at the "stuff" that makes up an educational organization—the physical plant; policies, plans, and procedures; systems for access control, accountability, discipline; and so on. Rather than dealing with specific individuals who are problematic or a potential threat, a vulnerability assessment examines and identifies potential problems with the physical surroundings and organizational documents.

A vulnerability assessment seeks to examine the discrepancy between what is written down—board-adopted policies, state requirements, local regulations—and what is actually done. Many times when we conduct vulnerability assessments we see this disparity very quickly. A school handbook might include a carefully detailed procedure for how visitors are signed in, yet in actuality the visitor sign-in log hasn't had an entry for weeks. Teachers can point to supervision schedules from the staff handbook, but the supervision doesn't typically occur, as other things "came up."

This disparity between theory and practice is often glaringly obvious. Think back to the district we discussed earlier that purchased the pricey system to screen visitors and scan their driver licenses. If asked about safety and security, the superintendent of that school district would probably respond that the district had a great system in place. On paper, it did. The reality of the situation, however, was very different.

At another district where we conducted a vulnerability assessment, the elementary, middle, and high schools were within a few short blocks of each

**FIGURE 2.1 |** Differences Between a Vulnerability
Assessment and a Threat Assessment

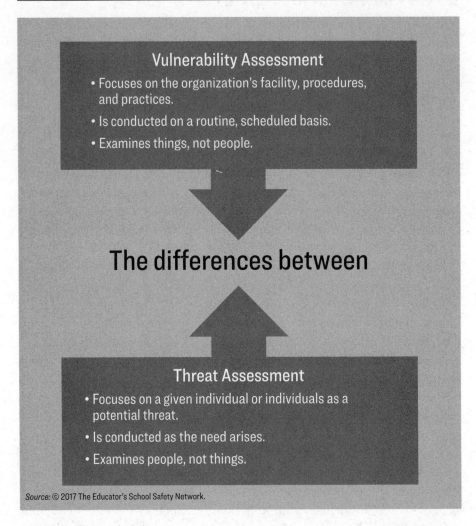

Source: © 2017 The Educator's School Safety Network.

other, and all dismissed their students at the same time. The district had an elaborate plan for the management and supervision of the more than 1,000 students leaving school and boarding 22 buses. What we observed was a very different scene. Instead of the 12 staff members who were slated to maintain peace and safety during this daily chaos, we saw only one harried principal and two staff members who were splitting their attention between the dismissal/bus-boarding activities and other urgent problems.

We watched in dismay as students poured out of the buildings, walked (or mostly ran) down the middle of the road, and chaotically converged onto a double line of idling buses that stretched for almost a block. The extensive supervision that was carefully detailed in the plan had long ago fallen by the wayside as teachers' schedules changed, staff members turned their attention to other dismissal concerns, and complacency resulted in people "forgetting" to fulfill their supervision duties.

The importance of an education-focused, comprehensive vulnerability assessment done by a fresh set of eyes that goes beyond a security perspective cannot be overstated. For many school administrators and decision makers, an objective, multifaceted assessment is the wake-up call that forces them to examine the way the school really runs every day—unlike a cursory walk-through to check to see if any doors are unlocked. We've done vulnerability assessment site surveys for schools that have already had walk-throughs by the local police or fire department. Although all the doors were locked and no fire code violations were present, there were still a myriad of dangerous safety, policy, supervision, and climate/culture issues that were identified only when looking at the school from the specific perspective of school safety. At one school, our discovery of a graffiti-laced wall and observation of students turned up a great hiding place behind the vending machine where students went to cut class. Another time, a casual conversation with a custodian led to the revelation that some students used the abandoned basement bomb shelter as a lunch hangout. At that same school, while standing outside watching the student parking lot, we noticed that a few students who did not have a first-period homeroom class waited at the locked entrance to let in their tardy friends, who snuck up the back stairwell—all while the school resource officer watched apathetically. If you are concerned about the safety of your school and want to jump-start the process, an interdisciplinary, multifactored vulnerability assessment is exactly the place to start.

## Intruder Assessments

Intruder assessments are a critical component of any multifactor vulnerability assessment, albeit a potentially uncomfortable and embarrassing one. The point of an intruder assessment is to determine how a potential intruder can gain access to the school and what areas that person is able to access once inside. When we conduct intruder assessments, we use a "professional intruder." This individual is not a trained spy, a paratrooper, or a con artist; she is another one of the Klinger kids, an artist by trade, who has no special skills in this area other than a friendly demeanor, a quick mind, and a complete lack of shame when confronted. When we conduct intruder assessments, we are not engaging in "gotcha journalism," attempting to "catch" a school being unsafe or unlocked. Rather, we are asked by the organization to test two critical components: access control and visitor engagement. Our intruder does not climb over a fence, rappel into a courtyard, or sneak in a window to gain access to the school; she walks in through an unlocked door, is let in by a student, or "tailgates" with other visitors being buzzed in. Despite the fact that the principal knows we are coming, our intruder's success rate in getting into a school is well over 99 percent, regardless of the type, age, size, or features of the facility. And that's not the scary part. The most frightening aspect of the intruder assessment is that, once inside, our intruder typically has unfettered access to the whole school.

As the assessment progresses, our intruder attempts to enter all the areas of the school, public and private, with the intent of eliciting some sort of interaction or response. She walks into occupied classrooms, through private offices, in and out of the mechanical and boiler rooms, and across crowded cafeterias—all in an attempt to get someone to notice that she shouldn't be where she is and assess what, if anything, to do about it. Again, regardless of the demographics, socioeconomic status, age, size, or population of the school, the results are shockingly similar. Pretty much everyone does pretty much nothing, even though many school faculty and staff observe someone they don't know moving through public and private areas of the school, encountering and interacting with staff and students.

Specific anecdotes of our intruder assessments are both shocking and scary. Our professional intruder once stood for more than 15 minutes in a lunchroom filled with 200 preschoolers, in full view of three staff members, and was not confronted. When someone finally asked what she wanted, she replied, "I'm just looking for my boyfriend's daughter," to which the aide replied, "Oh, OK," and walked away. Many times the school itself unwittingly assists this intrusion or provides information that puts students unnecessarily at risk. In one particular case, our intruder was wandering through a 2nd grade hallway and into a classroom of students taking a spelling test when a teacher asked her what she was doing there. She glanced at the signs posted in the hallway that showed the smiling students along with their names. Using that information, she quickly replied, "Oh, I'm Bailey Brown's aunt. You know, Bailey with the short curly black hair." The teacher immediately apologized for questioning her and allowed her to enter the classroom.

This is not just an elementary school issue; secondary schools can be equally problematic. Our intruder once walked through a propped-open door and found herself in the middle of a school assembly. No one reacted, so she went on to the vacant main office and took a selfie sitting in the principal's chair. In one memorable case, we were standing in the main office talking with the principal about the vulnerability assessment we were about to do. We looked up to see our professional intruder come out of the principal's office (he cordially greeted her!), go behind the main office counter, pull open a few file drawers with student records, pop into the nurse's office and rifle around in the medicine cabinet, and cheerily wave to us as she exited through the teachers lounge—all in full view of the oblivious secretary, attendance clerk, and guidance counselor. In virtually every site we assess, our intruder is able to enter "nonpublic" areas such as restrooms and boiler rooms without anyone—including the custodian sweeping the area—intervening. In this particular case, the custodian subsequently told us, "I was going to find out who you were and what you were doing after I got done sweeping the cafeteria."

Why doesn't anyone notice or take action? The lack of engagement could be because "this is a small school district; we know everyone." Well, they didn't know the professional intruder. Is the lack of action because no one saw the intruder? No, because our intruder always reports making eye contact with staff and often overhearing a hushed "Who is that?" Is this lack of action because the teachers are apathetic and don't care whether a stranger is among them? Not at all. Most of the time this is symptomatic of several issues we've already discussed:

- A highly centralized authority structure that suggests that it is the principal's job to identify and handle the intruder situation
- A lack of training and procedures that results in staff members feeling intimidated rather than empowered when it comes to dealing with potential intruders or related safety concerns

- Visitor-engagement procedures or supervision instructions that are written down but not actually implemented, most likely because no one ever explained the rationale and merely expected compliance rather than engagement

So, how do you avoid a situation that allows a stranger to have free rein in your school? First, establish a procedure *and* an expectation that everyone who collects a paycheck from the organization will participate in effective visitor engagement *every* time, *every* day, with *every* person they see. It's really a simple, free, and effective fix—"Good morning. How can I help you?"—but everyone has to do it. When all visitors (and potential intruders) are greeted by everyone they encounter and cheerily escorted to the place they are supposed to be—or at least back to the office to sign in—the result is a win-win. The confused community member feels welcomed and assisted while trying to find the library; helicopter parents learn they can't just "sneak in" to bring their child a forgotten homework assignment; and the would-be perpetrator who was intending to steal iPhones decides he is going down the street to the next school that doesn't engage with visitors. Once you've fixed the first item on the above list, you can address the second and third issues, which you'll learn more about in the coming chapters.

## Policy Review

A policy review is another education-specific aspect of a complete vulnerability assessment. When we do a policy review, we are essentially looking for one thing: the discrepancy between what is written down (the formal policy) and what is actually done (the informal procedure). As we've already stated, many schools have extensive policies that detail the way in which visitors are able to access the building; then we observe the reality— the visitor log hasn't been used in weeks, the badges can't be found, and the security camera for access control is "temporarily" not working.

This disconnect between what is "promised" by the board-approved policy and what is actually delivered by the untrained, unaware staff is dangerous on several levels. A policy that is adopted but ignored is more problematic than not having a policy at all because it demonstrates that the school or district understands and acknowledges the need for and value of a particular approach yet is unable or unwilling to actually make it happen. Without an assessment or a review, school leaders operate under the false assumption that their carefully crafted protocols are being used and that they work. Good administrators don't just assume that excellent instruction is taking place in each classroom; they evaluate and check. Yet most principals are woefully uninformed about who is signing out whom, where cars are parking, which doors are propped open for convenience, and which staff members don't show up to supervise dismissal.

### A Last Word About Vulnerability Assessments

Although we've discussed several critical components of a good vulnerability assessment (a walk-through or site survey, comparing protocols to actual practice, intruder assessments, and a policy review), there are other activities that should be undertaken to have a comprehensive, education-based vulnerability assessment. These items are listed in the *What Makes a Good Vulnerability Assessment* checklist found in the Resources section at www.eschoolsafety.org/resources.

## Threat Assessment: Who Should We Be Concerned About?

Threat assessment management (TAM) is a critical, effective, and long-lasting violence-prevention strategy that most schools really don't do—at least not well, which is frustrating. Threat assessment is defined by the U.S. Department of Education as "a fact-based, investigative approach to determining how likely a person is to carry out a threat of violence" (Vossekuil, Fein, Reddy, Borum, & Modzeleski, 2002). Based on our experiences in training educators, we define it as "the thing that teachers want the most." FEMA and the Department of Education go so far as to call threat assessment "one of the most useful tools a school can develop" (U.S. Department of Education, OESE, OSHS, 2013, p. 62).

Extolling the many merits of threat assessment and describing how best to implement and engage in it is an important conversation that far exceeds the length and breadth of this book. We must, however, in good conscience at least ensure a rudimentary understanding of what it is and why it is so critical to your school.

Unlike vulnerability assessment, threat assessment is not about stuff; it's about people. Threat assessment involves identifying, assessing, and managing individuals who may pose a threat to themselves or others. Threat assessment is done as the need arises—it can't be scheduled at the school's convenience. In threat assessment, an interdisciplinary team receives a referral and engages in a multidimensional, behavior-based investigation to determine if there are concerns about an individual, what the level of concern is, and what should be done about it. Think about the importance of the sentence you just read: This is a team that meets whenever it is needed, consisting of multiple disciplines (administration, teaching, mental health, law enforcement), to conduct an investigation and evaluation of facts and behaviors and then work collaboratively to identify and manage the potential for violence. Is this happening in an organized, systemic fashion in your school?

An understanding of threat assessment management centers on three critical verbs: *identify*, *assess*, and *manage*. Let's look at each of these in turn.

***Identify*** *individuals of concern who may pose a threat of violence to themselves or others.* A couple of other key words need some discussion. Any school stakeholder—student, parent, staff member, community member—could potentially be considered an individual of concern. Although the majority of times the focus may be on a student, it's important to keep a broader definition in mind. Then there's the dual focus of "themselves and others." Be sure not to narrow the focus. Threat assessment isn't just a means to identify the next school shooter. Conducted properly, threat assessment looks at all potential threats of violence or harm. Equal consideration needs to be given to behaviors that focus inward, such as suicide, self-harm, risk-taking behaviors, substance abuse, and so on, and those that present a threat to others, including dating violence, sexual assaults, fights, attacks, and, yes, shootings.

The "identify" aspect of threat assessment would seem to be the easy part. Teachers always tell us that they have a mental list of students who they are worried might be the ones to "shoot up the school." The difficulty, however, comes in getting referrals from staff members, teachers, parents, and peers who observe behaviors of concern and aren't quite sure what to do about them.

A few years ago, Amy was getting off a plane in Wyoming and received a frantic call from a principal in Wisconsin. He confided, "I'm holding a picture that one of my students drew of him stabbing his teacher in the head. Should I be concerned?" That principal had several critical problems. He clearly had an individual who was exhibiting a specific behavior of concern, but there was no formalized process to do anything about it. The principal was forced to essentially flip a coin and arbitrarily decide if the individual was a threat based on a single piece of information with no assistance, consultation, collaboration, or expertise. The existence of a TAM team in that Wisconsin school would have provided three things: (1) an investigation that yielded critical additional knowledge about the student from multiple perspectives, (2) a team of trained professionals who could collaboratively analyze the information they found, and (3) a carefully crafted and delineated process by which the level of concern could be authentically and accurately evaluated. Although we were happy to help and provide guidance, that principal would have been served far better by a TAM team in his own school.

*Assess* **the level of concern.** After the individual of concern has been identified, the TAM team makes a determination about the *level* of concern. How concerned should we be? Where is the individual on the pathway to targeted violence? The various models for a pathway to targeted violence (ideation, planning, preparation, implementation) come from the work of Fein and Vossekuil and of Calhoun and Weston and are presented in more detail in the Resources section at www.eschoolsafety.org/resources. Is the individual engaging in ideation or on the verge of implementation? Although all targeted violence needs to be addressed, an individual ready to implement a violent plan needs intensive intervention immediately. Remember that not every threat-assessment referral reveals a tangible, substantive, actionable threat. The vast majority of such referrals result in low-level (or no) intervention.

Assessing the level of concern is not based on how shocked or horrified you are by the threat. Trained TAM teams understand how to evaluate the specificity, plausibility, and validity of the threats they encounter. The fact that a referral turns out to be a low-level or nonconcerning threat doesn't mean that the threat-assessment process has failed. In fact, quite the opposite is true. The TAM team needs to be looking at all manner of threats in order to find the individuals who are actively engaged in planning, preparing, and implementing an act of violence (against themselves or others).

*Manage* **the individual of concern.** Here's where the process gets tricky (and sometimes misunderstood). Threat assessment is not a mechanism for kicking troubled kids out of school. The end goal of TAM is not to "get rid of" individuals of concern but rather to develop and implement supports, interventions, and systems that allow that individual to safely coexist with the rest of the people in the school.

Poorly prepared or trained TAM teams typically focus on identifying individuals of concern but omit or pay little attention to the critical work of providing appropriate supports and interventions. Any substantive threat should result in a management or care plan for that individual. Although this plan may incorporate counseling or other mental health services, a school can and should use other mechanisms in addition to or in concert with counseling. Making schedule changes, initiating no-contact policies, switching lunch tables, providing academic tutoring, meeting with parents and siblings, and incorporating coaches and extracurricular advisors are all small but important components of a comprehensive care plan that goes beyond just disciplinary action or mandated counseling. For additional information on providing supports and intervention, consult the *Tip Sheet for Intervention and Support* in the Resources section (available at www .eschoolsafety.org/resources).

We've worked with schools that endeavor to establish positive relation-ships with their students of concern by providing a mentor or instituting a daily check-in that ensures the student has several positive school-based interactions every day. Other programs that support conflict resolution, antibullying strategies, improving peer relationships, or other social-emotional connections are valuable tools.

The "manage" part of threat assessment raises one of the most funda-mental and troubling questions about school safety: How do we balance the right of individuals to a "free and appropriate public education" (or their rights as citizens to enter a public building) with the rights of the rest of the school stakeholders to be safe? How do we maintain the safety of the organi-zation while still advocating for or providing interventions to the troubled individual? The good news is that although this is still a difficult dilemma, a well-trained TAM team is effective at constructing and implementing care plans that balance these seemingly competing concerns.

The most central question that must be answered to ensure the safety of the school is whether an individual *made* a threat or *poses* a threat. Schools are very committed to identifying and punishing those who make a threat (such as words said in anger, inappropriate social media posts, or supposedly "funny" Instagram photos) yet have a blind spot when it comes to individuals who are engaging in behaviors that pose a threat.

An examination of past school shootings is often a tragic study of missed opportunities. The shooter at Arapahoe High School in Centennial, Colorado, kept a countdown of the days until his planned shooting in his agenda book, showed the gun he planned to use to multiple students, and verbally stated his intentions to students and staff alike, including the teacher he intended to kill (Goodrum & Woodward, 2016). The following key findings of the Safe School Initiative study demonstrate the critical need for threat assessment:

1. There was outward evidence of planning behaviors in more than 83 percent of all school shooters.
2. Attackers warned peers or siblings about the attack 93 percent of the time.
3. In 76 percent of the attacks, at least three people were concerned about the individual's behavior before the incident.
4. Attackers made verbal or written threats toward the target only 13 percent of the time. (Vossekuil et al., 2002)

In other words, those who are most likely to commit violence are demonstrating it through their behaviors and actions (posing a threat, as in #1 and #3 in the list), not just through their words (making a threat, as in #2 and #4 above). It would appear that potential perpetrators are begging someone to stop them, but no one is paying attention.

Perhaps the best explanation of the procedure and value of threat assessment is through the overhead projector analogy. Many of you reading this may have at one time either taught with (the old ones like Amy) or received instruction with (young whippersnappers!) an overhead projector. Think about the overhead transparencies you've seen. Back in the day, English teachers were always jealous of the "exciting" transparencies that the science department used to overlay the muscles on top of the skeleton, or the magma over the molten core. Approaching your thinking about students of concern in a similar way could be especially illuminating. What if you gave an overhead transparency to everyone who knows something about a particular student—one to friends, one to parents, one to teachers, one to coaches, one to the counselor—and asked them to list what behaviors they were concerned about? You might start out looking at a single list and think, "Oh, not so bad!" But when you overlay the concerns of all the different parties, the more complete profile that emerges may paint a very clear and alarming picture of behaviors that indicate a different level of concern. That's the beauty and value of threat assessment: It allows you to connect the dots and put together a clear, accurate picture not just of what someone says, but of what someone does—and how concerned you should be about it.

Perhaps one of the barriers to having active threat assessment in every school is that it requires the creation of a dedicated, trained interdisciplinary team. It cannot be effectively implemented in a piecemeal fashion. Further information on the effectiveness of threat assessment as well as specifics about setting up and training a threat assessment team are available in the Resources section at www.eschoolsafety.org/resources.

# Emergency Operations Plans

3

So far we've "set the table" with discussions about both why our schools are not safe enough and what we're trying to accomplish to make them safer. We've outlined how to analyze the potential threats and vulnerabilities your school faces. Now it's time to stop admiring the problem and do something about it—by creating an organized, systematic emergency operations plan, or EOP, for identifying and responding to incidents.

High-quality emergency operations planning is a substantial undertaking. This chapter provides an introduction to EOPs and the role of such plans in an education-based, comprehensive, all-hazards approach to school safety. Our focus will be on best-practice recommendations for reviewing or updating your existing plan, complying with specific state or local mandates, or starting from scratch. We'll discuss critical activities in the EOP planning process, such as the formulation of a multidisciplinary planning team, as well as best-practice recommendations for EOP components such as flip charts, incident command structures, response protocols, planning for recovery, and what are called "functional annexes" (plans related to broad tasks). We'll take you through the basic pieces of an EOP, but for a more complete understanding of the EOP process, or for further assistance in creating or revising an EOP, consult the Resources section for this chapter at the end of this book and go to www.eschoolsafety .org/resources.

The importance of a well-written, comprehensive EOP cannot be overstated. We can opine about the need for safer schools, purchase cutting-edge safety technology and apps, or passionately expound on our commitment to preventing violence, but it takes a formalized, strategic emergency operations plan created specifically for a given organization to go from a disjointed, abstract discussion to the implementation and application of solutions.

It is important to remember that the school community can be significantly affected even if a serious injury or death does not occur. Generally speaking, every school will experience some type of crisis incident nearly every school year. The crisis event may not be catastrophic, but failure to plan and prepare is simply not an option (FEMA, 2011).

## The EOP: What It Is and How It Often Falls Short

An emergency operations plan, often called a crisis plan, is defined by FEMA as a document that does the following:

- Assigns roles and responsibilities to groups and individuals for actions to be implemented during an emergency.
- Sets up lines of authority and how these actions are coordinated.
- Describes what will be done to protect people and property during crisis events.
- Identifies the resources to be used to provide that protection.
- Delineates steps for mitigation during response and recovery. (FEMA, 2010)

Emergency operations plans are constructed at the federal, state, and local levels by virtually all organizations, including schools. Although requirements for EOPs may vary from state to state, a good EOP addresses the specifics about who is assigned to do what under what circumstances in all phases of a crisis event or emergency. All EOPs should be comprehensive, addressing prevention, mitigation, response, and recovery using an all-hazards approach.

As shown in Figure 3.1, the U.S. Department of Homeland Security (DHS) defines preparedness as "a continuous cycle of planning, organizing, training, equipping, exercising, evaluating, and taking corrective action in an effort to ensure effective coordination during incident response" (U.S. Department of Homeland Security, 2017). As in our discussion of threat assessment in Chapter 2, there are some important verbs here, denoting activities in which not every school engages. In many states, the "plan" and "organize" phases are mandated by legislation requiring schools or districts to submit some sort of crisis plan. Typically, this legislation doesn't have any requirements regarding the active application phases of "train" and "exercise," so these steps occur much less frequently. It is also important to note that legislative requirements typically require only "compliance," meaning that as long as a school or district can "check the box" indicating that a plan was completed, the requirement is met. We have seen EOPs with plainly incorrect information, but because a plan was turned in to the state, the legislative requirement was met.

**FIGURE 3.1 |** Preparedness Cycle

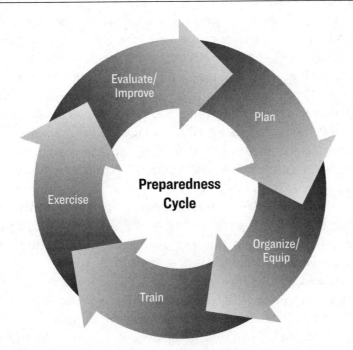

*Source:* From *Preparedness Cycle,* (2016), by Federal Emergency Management Agency (FEMA).

In addition, school leaders (or the unfortunate administrative intern put in charge of crisis plan revisions) typically feel ill-equipped to prepare and deliver training or to coordinate and implement exercises and drills. As founders of one of the few if not only nonprofit, education-based school safety organizations, we are constantly frustrated by the lack of training, drills, and opportunity to practice provided to educators.

Even worse, when training is left entirely up to law enforcement and is delivered exclusively from a law enforcement perspective, the drill or exercise becomes intimidating, frightening, and downright counterproductive for educators. School-based drills and exercises that are arranged and directed *by* emergency responders, *for* emergency responders often result in the educators being reduced to "props"—victims to be rescued or casualties to be triaged.

It is significant that the preparedness cycle is graphically illustrated by FEMA as a circle, not a linear process. As soon as an organization has moved through the cycle from planning to evaluation, it is time to start again. Although this approach is fairly common in virtually all emergency response organizations such as fire and police departments, it is often not the case in schools. Whereas most schools have at least a rudimentary crisis plan or EOP, our experience indicates that in many cases the process has stalled out early in the preparedness cycle (planning), as the EOP either needs major revisions (is more than two or three years old) or uses outdated protocols and lists of decision makers who don't even work for the school anymore. Even in districts with more up-to-date plans, the plan often is not specific to the organization (using boilerplate language borrowed from a template) or is overburdened with an unwieldy number of variations of the same type of incident—and not much else (failing to address all likely hazards).

This description of the shortcomings of many school EOPs may seem unnecessarily harsh, given the many demands on educators' time. But let's take a look at the problems inherent in a substandard crisis plan. One school that we recently consulted with had a plan that contained lists of individuals who were identified as key decision makers. The problem was that the plan had not been reviewed or revised for more than five years, and none of those individuals were still employed at the school. Several sections of the plan had clearly been borrowed from wherever the principal at the time had last worked, as they were cut and pasted in (with different formatting and inapplicable information). No one thought to remove the name of the original school, and the sections copied referenced an auditorium (this school didn't have one), a soccer field (didn't have that either), and a primary school located on the same campus (also not true). Finally, although the creators of the plan should get points for imagination, they spent a great deal of time writing extensive, repetitive protocols for virtually every crisis scenario they could conjure up. There were protocols for bomb threats on a bus, in the school, at the stadium, and so on. Procedures were outlined for what to do if a student was kidnapped, taken hostage, wandered away, ran away, or hid in the school.

Now let's think about how the EOP we've just described is actually *used*. A crisis event occurs. Frantic teachers grab the crisis plan to call for assistance because they aren't sure what to do—they haven't had any training or practice drills. Every phone number someone calls is incorrect, and no one recognizes any of the people listed who are supposed to decide what to do. One teacher finds a section of the plan that may help but is confused by the response directives that refer her to the auditorium or direct her to evacuate to the nearby kindergarten campus. In a panic, the teachers flip through pages and pages of detailed procedures, trying to discern which of the many scenarios listed are closest to what they are currently dealing with. Does this seem like an effective way to plan, prepare for, and respond to life-and-death events?

Recommendations from FEMA and DHS put equal emphasis not just on planning but also on training, equipping, exercising, and evaluating. These are areas that schools typically do not adequately address. Although we would be thrilled if a school had a good EOP that addressed prevention, mitigation, response, and recovery, if the plan just gathers dust on a shelf, then it doesn't much matter. After a plan is written, schools need to concern themselves with "living" it through training, organizing resources, drilling and exercising, and finally evaluating and revising.

## What an EOP Is Not

Now that we've defined what an EOP is, let's take a moment to reflect on what it is *not*. An EOP is not a boilerplate, fill-in-the-blanks template that is completed with grudging compliance to meet a seemingly arbitrary directive from some outside entity—although that is how many school communities typically view it. An EOP should not paint a picture of what we "theoretically" do in a crisis event; it should reflect the policies, practices, and procedures that are well established and understood by all stakeholders in the school and emergency response communities.

An EOP is not the same thing as a flip chart that acts as a quick emergency response cheat sheet. An EOP is a large, comprehensive document that encompasses the overarching approach to emergency operations. It is unnecessary and inappropriate for an EOP to hang on a classroom wall. A flip chart or emergency response cheat sheet is a succinct distillation of the response procedures contained in the EOP. A copy of the flip chart or cheat sheet should be easily accessible to everyone who works in a school because such a document is vital for quick reference while responding to a crisis event.

While we are talking about flip charts, here are a few important notes to keep in mind. Be picky about what goes into your flip chart. Many manufacturers sell laminated, durable flip charts that, although attractive, may not accurately represent the specifics or unique attributes of responding in *your* school. Remember that the content of a flip chart should be determined by your organization's school safety team, not the manufacturer. All too often, we see schools where the flip charts waste valuable space on threats that the manufacturer deemed important but that aren't necessarily critical or even applicable to the school. For example, if your school isn't in a flood-prone area, "flooding" shouldn't be on page one of your flip chart.

In general, flip charts should be easy—as in easily accessible, organized so that it's easy to find specific sections, and perhaps most important, easy to read (i.e., simple and concise). We've worked with schools where, in an effort to be comprehensive, completely accurate, and overly explanatory, a flip chart has been created that is almost impossible for the average person to use in the panic and chaos of a crisis event.

Focus on response procedures in your flip chart. We'll describe these procedures in more detail in Chapter 6, but for now, know that your flip chart should be organized by responses, not hazards. Separate pages for "bad guy in the neighborhood" and "severe weather" are redundant if the response for each event is to enact a reverse evacuation. A clear, concise listing of what you are trying to accomplish in a reverse evacuation will help a teacher in each of those scenarios and requires a lot less flipping and searching.

## The Purposes of an EOP

When done correctly, an emergency operations plan serves four critical purposes:

- Anticipates the likelihood of potential crisis events.
- Outlines roles, responsibilities, and duties related to prevention and response.
- Provides assurances of appropriate, adequate planning and preparation.
- Increases the organization's legal protections from liability. (FEMA, 2011)

Let's explore each of the purposes of an EOP in more detail.

### Anticipates the Likelihood of Potential Crisis Events

In Chapter 2 we talked about the need for schools to determine the type of threats that they may face through the use of vulnerability assessments (of which the intruder assessment forms a part) and threat assessment management. As part of effective EOP planning, decision makers need to examine not just the type of vulnerabilities or threats but also the relative likelihood that they will occur (their frequency) and the associated level of risk. A risk matrix of some sort is often used to examine the level of risk for a particular occurrence (see the example in Figure 3.2). These diagrams can range from brainstorming activities to more complicated matrices with complicated variables and calculations that determine probability and impact in a detailed fashion. Regardless of the level of sophistication or detail, it is critical to examine how often or frequently a threat or event occurs compared with its associated level of severity, impact, or consequence. An event that occurs frequently with a high level of impact or consequence needs to be a focus of the EOP. Conversely, a low-frequency, low-consequence event is of lesser importance but still needs to be considered in planning. We'll talk briefly about the use of the matrix here, but to complete the risk matrix for your school, see the *Risk Matrix Worksheet* located in the Resources section at www.eschoolsafety.org/resources.

**FIGURE 3.2** | Risk Matrix Worksheet Showing Levels of
Consequence and Frequency of Potential Crisis Events

|  | High Consequence | Moderate Consequence | Low Consequence |
|---|---|---|---|
| **High Frequency** |  |  |  |
| **Moderate Frequency** |  |  |  |
| **Low Frequency** |  |  |  |

*Source:* © 2017 The Educator's School Safety Network.

There are several important considerations to keep in mind when using this type of risk matrix. Where particular risks are plotted in the matrix varies widely based on factors such as the geography, demographics, facilities, and configuration of a given school. This is particularly true of weather-related events. For example, the frequency of tornados is different depending on where you are in the United States. Proximity to certain threats—such as a railway route for the transport of toxic chemicals, a valley prone to flash flooding, or a nearby prison—affects where on the threat matrix these items might be plotted. Conversely, some threats—such as an active shooter, a bomb incident, a noncustodial parent, or a medical emergency—are common to pretty much all organizations regardless of their unique locations or characteristics.

The rate of frequency of events can often be quantified fairly accurately by using local or regional crime statistics, meteorological data, and other objective measures. Frequency should not be determined by how long ago someone can remember an event occurring, or if the event happened in a neighboring district.

When completing a risk matrix, try to be as inclusive and wide-ranging as possible, taking into consideration less "dramatic" but equally problematic events such as extreme heat (the number-one cause of weather-related deaths), power outages, large-scale fights, bus accidents, and so on. Also be sure to consider both threats and events that may be specific only to the school and those that could be community-based but still affect the school. After completing the matrix, examine the level of attention and detail that is given in the EOP to threats or events that are high consequence and high frequency as compared to those that are low frequency and low consequence.

This discussion of detailing the frequency and severity of all the potential threats or incidents may seem contradictory to our statement earlier in the chapter about not having protocols for every imaginable scenario. The point is to determine what events are most likely to happen and would have the highest level of consequence, and to take steps not just to respond to them but also to make plans for prevention and mitigation. A proactive plan for preventing, minimizing, and deterring threats and incidents is a critical part of an EOP. Later in this chapter we'll discuss the basic response protocols that should be used to respond to the various threats outlined in the matrix.

## Outlines Roles, Responsibilities, and Duties Related to Prevention and Response

An effective EOP clearly outlines the responsibilities and duties of all school staff members, not just key decision makers. By delineating specific responsibilities, staff members understand the activities that they must undertake during a crisis event, empowering and enabling them to protect the lives of their students, their colleagues, and themselves. The key here is not just listing these job functions but ensuring that those to whom these duties have been assigned have been informed and given appropriate, ongoing training specific to what they are supposed to do. Let's take a look at some examples that typify this important element:

- The custodian who daily monitors and controls the boiler, air conditioning, and other utilities should be the person assigned to shut down the HVAC systems during a chemical spill with a shelter-in-place protocol or to turn off the gas after a tornado damages the building.
- A classroom teacher whose daily responsibilities include supervising students, taking attendance, and providing instruction should have a similar role in a crisis event, such as moving the students to safety, accounting for everyone, and providing emotional comfort and support.
- A dean of students with advanced first-aid training and past military experience is a good choice to direct triage in a mass-casualty event, or to be stationed outside to meet responders or others who arrive in response to a crisis incident.

- The secretary who knows everyone is well suited to checking in parents at the reunification site after a traumatic event.

Although clearly the skills and dispositions of these individuals may vary, where EOP roles and responsibilities are concerned, two things are critical:

- Staff members must know exactly what the expectations are for their assigned roles and must be trained in how to complete them.
- There must be adequate redundancy (meaning backup people assigned to the same role) so that, for example, when the custodian is unavailable, someone else knows how to shut off the water.

When specific crisis-response procedures are delegated to staff members—and more important, those individuals have been adequately trained and empowered to perform these functions—confusion and chaos are minimized and these critical activities are much more likely to be performed during a crisis event. This point underscores the fact that an EOP cannot be a binder that collects dust on a shelf. It is a critical component of a school's safety work.

A comprehensive EOP can also educate other school stakeholders, such as students, parents, and community members, about their roles during a crisis event, allowing the energies, efforts, and abilities of those who want to help to be more effectively leveraged. Provisions that speak to issues of concern to parents, such as communication, reunification, and accountability for students, are particularly important and should be discussed with stakeholders in advance rather than during the tension and chaos of the actual event.

## Provides Assurances of Appropriate, Adequate Planning and Preparation

A clear plan for effectively responding to crisis events that is adequately communicated to all school stakeholders provides evidence and assurance of both planning and preparation. In addition to preparedness, this assurance has a positive effect on school climate and helps foster a feeling among students that the school is a safe place to learn. An EOP also helps alleviate fears about what to do when a crisis occurs, keeps people calmer and more focused, and ultimately helps save lives.

Although every school employee needs information about roles and responsibilities in a crisis event, it isn't necessary for every person to have intimate knowledge of the entirety of the EOP. School administrators and leaders will need more granular knowledge and more familiarity due to their heightened role in crisis response. Although we are in no way advocating that every detail of a crisis plan be made available to parents and community members, school stakeholders (including students) need to be aware that there is a plan, that it is well thought out and ready to be executed, and that they have a role to play as well.

## Increases the Organization's Legal Protections from Liability

The legal requirements for an EOP vary widely from state to state, and what is required of public schools is different from what is required of independent or private schools, so a discussion of legal requirements isn't feasible here. Broadly speaking, in all school safety matters, courts will require that the conduct and policies of the school be "reasonable" under the circumstances. It is flatly unreasonable for a school or school district not to plan for crisis events. It is heartening that this is one area where the legal responsibilities of educators and school leaders align exactly with the moral imperative to keep kids safe.

Well-reasoned policies that make a good-faith attempt to keep kids safe at school will not only have a positive impact on school safety but will also diminish a school's legal liability. Therefore, improvement in the area of emergency operations planning serves these twin aims. Neglecting or delaying addressing these obligations can leave a school open to incredible levels of legal liability. It is important that the perfect not become the enemy of the good; an EOP can be incrementally improved and updated—it need not be perfect to protect life and diminish liability. Refer back to the preparedness cycle described earlier in this chapter; every time an EOP moves through the cycle from planning to evaluation, it improves. The critical activity is to engage in the cycle to begin with (i.e., create an adequate EOP) and to engage in continuous improvement moving forward. This concept of *plan, instruct, assess, evaluate,* and *revise* is certainly not new to any educator; it is the bedrock of everything we do pedagogically.

We strongly recommend having a building- or district-level safety team (or both) that undertakes the work of crisis management and response in an ongoing fashion. It's important to note that we are not talking about a threat assessment team; these are not the folks to whom teachers refer students of concern. Instead, this team works (not just occasionally, but continually) on safety activities such as assessing vulnerabilities, creating/revising the EOP, and implementing the program (via training, facility modifications, drills, etc.).

Even if an EOP is not required by law, the creation, implementation, and execution of an EOP is undeniably a best practice because an organized, systematic plan for identifying and responding to incidents serves many important functions in addition to the preservation of life and property. Perhaps most important, the school has a moral and legal responsibility to care for students in a crisis event when parents cannot. School decision makers have a legal obligation to ensure adequate safety planning and precautions related to disasters. Neglecting this obligation leaves school leaders open to personal and systemic liability for damages, injuries, and deaths that occur at the school. Creating and implementing an effective EOP increases legal protections from liability and can be used to defend the district if litigation follows a crisis event (Dorn & Dorn, 2005).

## The EOP Planning Team

The first step in developing or revising an EOP is to form a planning team. There is strong consensus in the world of emergency planning, from FEMA on down, that this team should be multidisciplinary. Although emergency responders such as police, fire, or EMS personnel immediately come to mind, the team should also include special education directors, counselors, school nurses, maintenance/custodial personnel, and other school stakeholders. In some cases, the safety team is tasked with implementing what the EOP planning team creates; in other cases, the safety team *is* the EOP planning team. The critical concern is the ability and willingness to collaborate among the various agencies that will find themselves responding to a crisis event in a school.

A firefighter related a great example of this to us recently when he described what happened when his unit responded to a minor fire at an elementary school. The well-intentioned 2nd grade teachers decided to choose a spot outside the building where students would gather after an evacuation so that they could be accounted for. This was a good example of planning, right? Unfortunately, the spot they chose was at the fire hydrant in front of the building. The firefighters arrived on the scene and had to move 92 8-year-olds before they could hook up the hoses. Interagency planning in the EOP process would have prevented this response delay.

Of equal concern is the tendency for educators to abdicate their decision-making capabilities during the planning process. Although the input of trained emergency responders is critical, the plan itself needs to address crisis response in a specialized environment (a school) with uniquely trained (or untrained) individuals. As educators, we do not presume to know exactly how the fire services or police department works, so why would we assume that those same individuals understand the unique constraints and capabilities of an educational setting? To have a truly collaborative planning team, the team members must acknowledge, and defer to, the specific knowledge, skills, and dispositions of *all* the different disciplines that are required to adequately respond to a crisis event—not just the emergency responders.

During one EOP consultation, we advocated vigorously for collaboration with the local fire and police departments in a town where this relationship had become politicized and strained. When we finally were able to bring the multiple agencies together with the school, the misconceptions and misunderstandings were quickly apparent. After discussions that provided everyone with an opportunity to talk, the fire chief found out that he had a fundamental misunderstanding and underestimation of the challenges associated with the medically fragile students in the school's classroom for students with multiple disabilities. Conversely, school administrators learned that an evacuation route they thought was not available to them because it would involve crossing a busy street actually could be used because law enforcement could easily close the street, resulting in a more rapid, effective evacuation of students. Without interagency collaboration, these problems (and benefits) would have been actualized only in the chaos and trauma of a crisis event.

The EOP planning team has a specific and limited job—to develop and evaluate a plan for emergency response that incorporates prevention and mitigation, planning, response, and recovery. Once the plan has been completed, it is up to all school stakeholders to acquire the appropriate knowledge about the EOP. The planning team is not a rapid-response, in-the-field squad (that is more typically a crisis-response team) or a long-term implementation committee (such as a district- or building-level safety team). Instead, the planning team is a knowledgeable, interdisciplinary group of professionals with the specific goals, expertise, and resources to create and evaluate a comprehensive, all-hazards emergency operations plan for the school. Team members need to act as planners and evaluators, not implementers or trainers. In later chapters we will talk about the critical role of safety teams in implementing, maintaining, and evaluating the crisis plan.

Incident command structure (ICS) is the universal "language" of command and organization that all institutions and agencies are encouraged or required to adopt. The incident command structure provides a common organizational framework of "who does what," which makes it easier for agencies to cooperate. Figure 3.3 shows an example of such a structure.

The creation of universal incident command stemmed from the difficulty agencies had in trying to cooperate their response during 9/11. Fire, law enforcement, and EMS agencies were organized in dissimilar ways, which made their prolonged cooperation and communication needlessly difficult. The EOP should use the incident command structure to manage all incidents and in all phases of incident management, from planning to recovery (FEMA, 2011).

Schools are encouraged to adopt ICS so that when emergency responders respond to a crisis event at a school, the organizational structures of the two institutions are compatible and cooperation can happen under duress. Firefighters or police officers should not have to talk with 10 different school staff members to find out who is the school's incident commander. In addition, when the principal is not at the school (applying Murphy's Law—"Anything that can go wrong, will go wrong"—to crisis events), there should still be a clear chain of command with redundancy as to who is working in unified command with responders.

Although it may not be the most thrilling professional development you've ever undertaken, FEMA offers a free online, on-demand course (IS-100.SCA: Introduction to the Incident Command System for Schools) that provides an important overview of the use of incident command in school-based events. You can find the link to IS-100.SCA in the Resources section at www.eschoolsafety.org/resources.

**FIGURE 3.3 |** Incident Command Structure

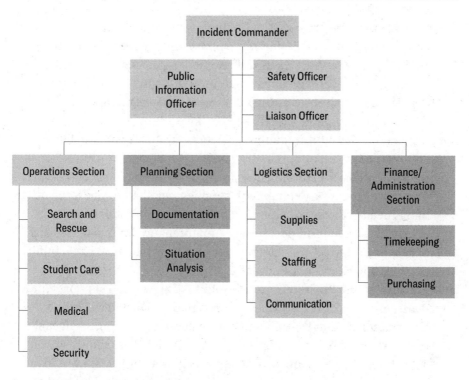

Source: © 2017 The Educator's School Safety Network.

The good news is that ICS isn't that different from the way schools are typically organized. Understanding ICS is not a matter of creating new departments or hiring new employees, but of thinking differently about the personnel and resources already in place. The ICS staffing is typically organized into the following sections:

- **Management: The "decision makers."** The management section is composed of the incident commander and supporting staff in charge of making decisions during the crisis event response and recovery. Management functions should be assigned to school staff members who already fulfill managerial roles, such as building-level or district-level administrators or, for the sake of redundancy, to those in pseudo-administrative roles like athletic directors, guidance counselors, supervisors, or directors (Kentucky Center for School Safety, 2016).

- **Operations: The "doers."** Individuals in the operations section perform the actual tasks during response and recovery. Depending on the tasks required, school staff members from both the certified and classified sides typically would fulfill these functions (Kentucky Center for School Safety, 2016). The most obvious members of the operational section are those who have direct contact and responsibilities with students—teachers, paraprofessionals, bus drivers, and other support staff.
- **Logistics: The "getters."** Those in the logistics section acquire and manage the necessary equipment, supplies, perishable goods, and other things needed during response and recovery. School staff members involved in student support services, maintenance and custodial staff, and those in clerical and secretarial positions would most likely fulfill this function (Kentucky Center for School Safety, 2016).
- **Planning: The "thinkers or planners."** This section supports the management section by thinking through the plan and gathering information so that the incident commander and support staff can make informed decisions. Building- and district-level administrators, department heads, team leaders, and other teacher leaders would be appropriate personnel to fulfill this function (Kentucky Center for School Safety, 2016).
- **Finance: The "record keepers."** The finance section keeps complete records and is fiscally accountable for expenses incurred during response and recovery. Staff members in the treasurer's or accounting offices would most likely fulfill this function (Kentucky Center for School Safety, 2016). For more education-specific information on incident command, see *What Does ICS Look Like in Schools?* in the Resources section at www.eschoolsafety.org/resources.

One final note: as we have pointed out, educators are the "first" first responders, and the principal or key decision maker must be the incident commander when an incident begins in a school. However, we need to acknowledge that when the crisis event extends beyond or overwhelms the capabilities of the school, requiring the presence of law enforcement, medical, or fire emergency responders, then the incident command responsibilities must also shift to allow those responders to do their jobs. If your school has experienced a violent event, then most likely law enforcement officials will take command of the incident upon their arrival. When the school is on fire, the fire chief, not the principal, is in charge. In an active shooting event, law enforcement officials will be the incident commanders. This delegation of authority is not always as cut and dried as it may seem, depending on the nature and circumstances of the crisis event. What about when a bomb threat has been found written in a restroom stall, or when a cafeteria fight gets out of hand? Will law enforcement alone be making all the decisions about response, investigation, and disposition? Most likely it will be a collaborative effort. Both school and emergency-responder decision makers must be prepared to work jointly, but ultimately there will need to be one incident commander—and in cases where the event is beyond the capability of the school, educators need to be ready to lead in emergency responders' absence and then turn decision making over to them.

## EOP Components

The EOP itself consists of three components: (1) the basic plan, (2) functional annexes, and (3) hazard-specific appendixes. Here are the basic elements of each:

- **Basic plan.** The basic plan provides a big-picture view of the plans for emergency response in the school or district. The plan delineates emergency response authority, lists the nature of the crisis events addressed, and outlines the roles and responsibilities of those responding. The basic plan is the section of the document where the rationale, parameters, and organizational structure of the EOP are established and explained. This section is in many ways the housekeeping section of the document, where the theory, structure, and limitations of the plan are established.

- **Functional annexes.** The plans that "describe the actions, roles, and responsibilities of participating organizations" (FEMA, 2010, p. 3-5) are called functional annexes. Each annex is dedicated to one of the critical emergency response functions that must be performed. Functional annexes are the working sections of the EOP, where individuals can locate and understand what their roles and responsibilities are in a given situation. Although there may be general concepts that are common from one functional annex to the next (e.g., the teacher's responsibility to account for all students), there are also tasks that may be unique to a particular functional annex, such as moving students under their desks in a "drop, cover, and hold" response.

- **Hazard-specific appendixes.** These appendixes are more detailed than functional annexes and provide information specific to a particular hazard. They are typically attached to the relevant functional annex. The hazard-specific appendixes provide additional guidance and specific functions that are dictated by the nature of the event (FEMA, 2010). For example, a severe-weather annex may address moving students into the building from outside areas, and a hazard appendix that is specific to tornadoes may outline activities such as moving students into first-floor interior hallways, away from windows.

You will find detailed descriptions and additional information on specific EOP components in *Components of Comprehensive School and School District Emergency Management Plans* in the Resources section at www .eschoolsafety.org/resources, though we remind you not to copy and paste, and instead tailor the examples to your specific needs.

## The Process of Developing an EOP

The work of emergency planning is complex and varied, but it is a necessity if you are to make your school safer for your students. A good first step in tackling this important task is to have a working knowledge of the process that must be undertaken to develop an effective all-hazards, comprehensive EOP. In general, an interdisciplinary EOP planning team needs to work through each of the following steps in the process:

1. The team needs to begin by researching and reviewing the unique circumstances, attributes, and vulnerabilities of the school in order to do the following:
   - Understand the hazards, resources, demographic characteristics, and limitations of the school. Local, state, and federal requirements should be reviewed, including existing mutual aid agreements and memorandums of understanding.

- Identify potential hazards, vulnerabilities, and risks that must be addressed in the EOP, including frequency, scope, severity, and consequences.
- Develop mitigation efforts to address these hazards and vulnerabilities.

2. Next, the team takes the information found in its review and research and applies it to develop and write the plan, which should include the following:
   - Basic plan.
   - Functional annexes.
   - Hazard-specific appendixes.

3. When the team has finished creating the plan, its work is not done. It is critical to validate the plan through reviewing and testing. The team must do the following:
   - Ensure that the EOP conforms to required regulations and requirements, and more important, that it is useful in actual practice.
   - Facilitate a review of the plan by related state or local agencies, such as the local EMA or FEMA regional offices, in addition to local first responders. The final plan should be evaluated by key representatives of each associated organization through table-top or other functional exercises.

4. After EOP implementation, the team facilitates the movement of the plan through the preparedness cycle described earlier in this chapter. This maintains the plan as a living document.
   - When problems arise, situations change, deficiencies are noted, or regulations are altered, the planning team must adjust and incorporate these variables into the EOP through a formalized remediation or revision process.

Many additional activities, initiatives, and procedures can support and enhance the development and implementation of EOPs. Although there isn't room for a discussion of them here, please see the Resources section at www.eschoolsafety.org/resources for a list of suggestions, samples, and links for items such as emergency signage, EOP formats, and "To Go" bags.

## The Recovery Component

The aftermath of a crisis incident requires a shift to a new phase of action, "recovery," and it too must be incorporated into the EOP. The following sections explain this phase. (See Chapter 8 for more detailed coverage of the recovery process.)

### What Is Recovery?

Recovery consists of all the things that are done to return an organization to "normal." Recovery does not begin in the hours or days following a traumatic event; it begins when the response to the incident ends. When the intruder is taken away in handcuffs, the ambulance pulls away with the patient, the tornado warning is cancelled, or the gas leak is stopped, the school can stop responding and start recovering. The purpose of recovery planning and activities is to reestablish physical safety, satisfy basic human needs, and begin the process of physical and psychological healing in a movement toward normalcy after a crisis.

Recovery was critical at a nearby school when a tornado destroyed nearly all of the district's schools. The process of recovery from that event began in the dark, in the pouring rain that followed the tornado, as the superintendent worked with responders to secure the scene of the wreckage from curious onlookers. It continued with the vast "to-do" lists that included items such as planning graduation from a high school that no longer physically existed, memorializing those who died, documenting the claim for insurance, arranging for staff members to recover items from the rubble, and providing grief counselors and mental health support. This organization's recovery from that devastating event was long and arduous, but it was ultimately successful. Thanks to the leadership of the administration; the commitment of the staff, students, and parents; and the resiliency of the community, the school district survived—and thrived.

We have worked with other schools that faced events that were less traumatic, such as a near-miss abduction or a bus accident that "could have been a lot worse," but still struggled to return to normalcy, even though the demands of reestablishing physical and emotional safety were significantly less. What are some of the factors that enhance an organization's recovery? Among them are a comprehensive view of what recovery activities are required and the advance planning and preparation to carry them out.

Recovery activities are not just counseling or mental health services. Recovery activities must begin by first meeting basic physical needs for first aid, water, food, and shelter (Brock et al., 2009). Depending on the nature of the event, a reorganization or change of the school environment may need to occur, such as gathering all students together, moving to a different location, or bringing police or security personnel onsite (Brymer et al., 2006). Recovery consists of a variety of mental health, operational, debriefing, and communication activities designed to return students to a safe school environment, reestablish the physical and psychological safety of all school stakeholders, and improve mitigation, planning, and response activities for future incidents. This process begins in the minutes after a crisis event and can last, quite literally, for years.

## What Happens When You Don't Plan for Recovery?

Recovery planning is often the forgotten stepchild of the EOP, as it is either absent or marginalized in school safety planning. We have seen many seemingly comprehensive, all-hazards crisis plans that cover almost every conceivable type of incident yet do not speak to the critical need for recovery. That's because there are competing interests that often supersede adequate recovery planning and training. This competition manifests itself as a failure to allocate some of the limited available resources to crisis recovery. The rationale is often that there isn't enough time, money, or personnel to adequately plan and prepare for the crisis events themselves, so how can consuming some of these resources for the "touchy-feely" process of recovery be justified? Isn't it more critical to at least be able to respond effectively to the event itself and worry later about cleaning up the mess, if it ever comes to that?

In the current prevalent view of school safety, planning for and responding to crisis events is primarily a law enforcement or emergency response activity. Recovery, then, is considered a "soft" skill that falls under the seemingly less valuable purview of education, mental health, and other support services. This misguided approach focuses on preventing or responding to an event but does not address the critical need to reestablish physical and psychological security and a return to normalcy. Part of the problem is a lack of understanding about what recovery is and why it is so critical.

**Planning for Recovery**

To be equipped to undertake critical recovery activities, schools must prepare and plan to recover. The EOP planning team must consider recovery as a part of the EOP that is equal to prevention and response, and create specific language, practices, and protocols to address the recovery needs discussed in this chapter.

We also recommend that each school create a recovery team that will be trained and equipped to implement the recovery activities incorporated into the EOP by the planning team. To do this, the school must determine the following:

- **Who should be on the team?** Individuals who are known to the students and have nurturing, supportive dispositions, as well as the capacity to remain calm under stress, are excellent candidates.
- **What responsibilities will the team have?** Specific roles and responsibilities should be assigned for both short- and long-term recovery activities. The recovery team should be oriented toward supporting school stakeholders, not completing operational or administrative activities.
- **What are the functions of the team?** Because there is a limited number of people on the team, one important function is to lead, facilitate, and support the rest of the school staff in undertaking recovery activities.
- **What resources both within the school and in the community will be provided?** The recovery team should coordinate the deployment of physical resources and personnel available in the school and through community-based agencies and organizations.

## Final Thoughts

For both philosophical and practical reasons, it isn't sufficient or wise to have an emergency operations plan that abdicates all responsibility to law enforcement or fire/emergency services. A crisis event in a school requires a very specific set of planning, response, and recovery capabilities that educators alone possess. An EOP developed for a different organization that is "retrofitted" for an educational institution is a square peg in a round hole. A school's EOP must reflect the unique attributes, vulnerabilities, and circumstances that exist only in educational organizations—and we as educators must put in the hard work to make it so.

Large-scale disasters will overwhelm normal emergency response agencies and disrupt existing infrastructures, requiring schools to respond to these events on their own for long periods of time (FEMA, 2011). Even if a crisis event doesn't negate the capabilities of emergency responders, it will take them time to respond. Schools must be ready to take care of themselves. Therefore, it is critically important that an EOP include specific protocols and plans beyond waiting for others.

# Practicing and Living the Plan 4

We begin this chapter with a note from Amy's experience:

> While I didn't teach in a one-room schoolhouse made of sod on the windswept frontier, I have been an educator for a long time. In the mid-1980s, when I was just starting out, there was little worry and even less conversation about crisis events in schools and what to do about them. Back then, when an irate parent whose son failed my English class (twice) and was ineligible to play football came across the table to attack me, it was my husband, not my principal, who was most upset.

In fact, in the early 1990s, when school violence was increasing (or perceived to be increasing), there was still pushback from teachers, some of whom vigorously maintained, "If I wanted to do safety work, I would have become a cop." Then the shooting at Columbine happened, and high school teachers saw things differently. The next decade saw a shift, especially in secondary schools, with increasing emphasis on (but mostly fear about) what to do in a crisis event. Then Sandy Hook happened. A week or so after this unthinkable event, we were doing a training in a small rural school district. Two kindergarten teachers came up to chat during the break. They were somewhat embarrassed to relate that they never used to think too much about school safety or an active shooter because it was a "high school" problem. Now, they tearfully confided, "We don't think like that anymore."

So, what does it take for the shift to be complete—from ignorance and apathy, to fear and anxiety, to confidence and empowerment? It takes practicing and living the plan.

This chapter builds on the discussion of emergency operations plans in Chapter 3 to examine how to best implement and practice the EOP in the daily operational activities of the school. We'll start with a discussion about the shifting of thinking and priorities that leads to establishing safety as a daily operational procedure that is not the sole responsibility of a lone administrator, but rather an important daily activity in all aspects of the school. This chapter examines specific strategies for empowering, not intimidating, school stakeholders so they can integrate safety procedures into their everyday work. Finally, we'll take a look at the importance and potential pitfalls of training and drills for all school stakeholders, along with specific suggestions for effective, appropriate training and exercising of the EOP.

Although the creation of an all-hazards, comprehensive emergency operations plan is vitally important in keeping schools safe, the most critical change that improves safety in a school is when all school stakeholders consider safety as a daily operating procedure, woven into the decisions, routines, and very foundation of every school day. This requirement doesn't mean that educators must be hypervigilant, constantly worried about danger instead of long division. Safety does not need to be the sole focus of staff or students at the expense of all else, which is an unrealistic and counterproductive notion. After all, you are running a school, not a prison. Instead, safety is the foundation upon which all the other work of education takes place. Educators who have been empowered and trained to respond appropriately and effectively to crisis events make decisions that are informed, but not ruled, by their school safety skills and knowledge. When school safety is incorporated as a daily operating procedure of a school, the empowerment and skills of stakeholders become a positive force in the climate and culture—and a powerful crisis-prevention measure.

## Critical Paradigm Shifts

For school safety to become an integral part of a school, a few key paradigms must be shifted. The first is an awareness and understanding of school safety as an education-based issue. Working to keep kids safe and supported in schools isn't "a safety issue that happens to take place in a school"; it is "a school issue that happens to involve safety." This might seem to be a subtle semantic distinction, but the effects are huge. When crisis response is viewed as a safety issue that just happens to take place in schools, there is a tendency to defer entirely to the judgment and decisions of law enforcement and other emergency responders. A one-size-fits-all approach to violence prevention and crisis response is misguided and ineffective. A response protocol that works in a more typically adult environment, such as an office building or a retail space, may be grossly inappropriate or even dangerous when applied to the unique concerns and constraints of a school. The most effective approach to school safety is one that is led by educators themselves, who collaborate with and incorporate the expertise of emergency responders.

Another critical shift is to organize school safety work in a way that is proactive, not just reactionary. Too often, schools and school districts place school safety on the back burner until there is a crisis event that must then be addressed. Planning and preparing for crisis events, working to prevent violence in schools, and proactively building safe and supportive environments is more effective, reduces anxiety in students and educators, and is ultimately cheaper (often, considering the costs of lawsuits, significantly so). School stakeholders must overcome the old mentality that school safety need not be addressed until a problem occurs.

It is human nature to focus on what is perceived to be most demanding of time and attention, but school safety training that addresses only active shooter response ignores the myriad of both human-caused and natural threats and crisis events faced by schools. It is tragic and unacceptable that children die in active shooter events in schools, but that doesn't mean it is the only crisis event for which schools must prepare. Without proper planning and training, students are in significant danger due to lack of access control in a school, failure to respond appropriately to medical emergencies, poorly handled bomb threats, or needlessly scary emergency response drills. Active shooter response must become one part of a comprehensive, all-hazards approach to school safety.

## Ensuring That Everyone Has a Role to Play

As we explained in the last chapter, it is critical that everyone understand that they have a role to play in "living" the plan. As noted earlier, in the past teachers often complained that "if I wanted to go into law enforcement, I'd have become a cop" when faced with responsibilities and expectations for safety. After the horrific tragedies of Virginia Tech and Sandy Hook, we no longer hear that refrain from educators. In fact, we hear quite the opposite. We frequently encounter school staff members who are frightened and frustrated by the lack of training they have been given. It's critical that school staffs transition from "I don't want to think about that" to "I know what to do." This shift occurs only when sufficient planning, preparation, *and* training occur.

The first step in redefining the roles of educators as responders is to overcome the fallacy that school safety is the principal's job. This notion comes from a highly centralized (and now highly outdated) approach to school safety. In the past, one person (the principal) received some safety training (usually from a law enforcement perspective), which was then expected to "trickle down" to the rest of the staff. In this centralized approach, the rest of the school staff have little if any training, don't understand what their specific roles and responsibilities are in a crisis event, and most dangerously, when faced with a crisis event, wait for instructions from the building leader before acting.

The dangers of this mindset were tragically illustrated in the Our Lady of the Angels fire in Chicago in 1958. After a fire was set in the basement bathroom, the building began to fill with smoke. Because there had not been training in fire evacuation, teachers on the third floor waited for instructions on how to respond until it was too late for them to evacuate. Due to inaction and lack of training, 92 children and 3 teachers died in the fire (Cowan & Kuenster, 1996).

We look back at this horrific loss of life and wonder, how could they just sit in their classrooms and wait? It seems so obvious that teachers would lead their students to safety at the first indication of smoke and fire. But that "obvious" attitude is due, in large part, to fire code regulations and mandated fire-evacuation training drills enacted after this tragedy in the hopes of ensuring that virtually every student and staff member would know what to do in a fire.

Sadly, the standardized, comprehensive commitment to fire safety and fire evacuation in schools doesn't carry over to other types of school safety incidents. Today, the lack of training and outdated protocols leave many teachers and students in exactly the same position as those in the Our Lady of the Angels fire: uncertain what to do, not knowing how to respond, and feeling vulnerable and afraid while waiting for someone to tell them how to save their lives.

Earlier we discussed the philosophical need to decentralize the authority to respond to and make life-and-death decisions in school crisis events. There are compelling practical reasons as well. If the person who makes all the decisions on how to respond to a crisis event is the building principal—a person likely to be unavailable, injured, or killed in the violent event—the staff must resort to "making it up" without training or guidance. In addition, the physical space containing most of the resources needed for crisis response is often the main office and—you guessed it—the most likely location to be compromised in the event, again leaving staff without the resources they need.

But just decentralizing authority and telling staff members that they must "make decisions now" is not enough. In fact, it can be counterproductive and outright dangerous without adequate, appropriate planning and training. If you are going to tell staff members that they must decide what to do in a crisis event, then you absolutely must give them the training and knowledge to make those decisions. In addition, school stakeholders need assistance in making the necessary shift, not just in unlikely but high-profile events such as school shootings, but also in the day-to-day work of keeping a building safe.

School administrators have several important roles in the work of school safety. Administrators are often asked to make critical decisions, guide the work of other faculty and staff, and serve as the public face of the school. However, one of the most important school safety duties of administrators is to foster and support the culture that believes that school safety is everyone's job. The challenges of creating such a culture are illustrated in a photo that we use in training school administrators. The photo depicts a door in a school labeled "Fire Door." On the fire door is an additional handmade sign that reads "Fire Door—Do not prop open." The photo clearly shows that the fire door is indeed propped open—with a fire extinguisher. In addition to appreciating the irony of this particular photo, we ask administrators which type of staff they currently have—one in which staff members walk by, see the door propped open, and think, "Well, there must be a reason it's open, and it's not my job," or one in which staff say, "That shouldn't be open," and close the door. Administrators must endeavor to create a culture where all school staff know that they have a role to play and are empowered to do something about it—which has applications far beyond the fire door.

There is an important distinction to be made here between educators who are empowered to do the daily work of school safety and those who are intimidated by it. In our work we often see educators who have a copy of the crisis plan, have sat through active shooter training, and maybe even serve on safety committees, but who are intimidated, not empowered, by their experiences. When policies, procedures, and training come solely from a law enforcement rather than an educational perspective, teachers are less confident and more frightened as a result. Embracing a purely law enforcement view of planning for, preventing, and responding to violence can sometimes intimidate rather than empower educators, and as a result, makes training and response significantly less effective. Do safety practices in your school empower or intimidate? Take the *Empower Not Intimidate* self-assessment located in the Resources section at www.eschoolsafety.org to find out.

Safety planning and training should not be primarily reactionary, but rather proceed in a targeted, proactive fashion. We see this shortcoming almost daily in our work. Schools are complacent or unprepared until a major incident occurs, followed by a flurry of activity and reminders of safety protocols for a short period, followed by a total lack of interest until the next event occurs—and then the cycle continues. It is up to building leaders to make safety an ongoing part of daily operations. One way to do this is to create a culture in the building where safety issues are considered year-round by all staff. We highly recommend that a specific safety item be placed on the agenda at every staff meeting. Doing so sends the message that safety is an everyday consideration and also allows for training, planning, and discussion to be ongoing. Keep in mind that we aren't suggesting a 30-minute lecture on tornado safety, but rather a 5-minute review of the established tornado plan, with time for questions and clarification.

## Redundancy

In all types of safety planning, one important area that is typically over-looked is that of redundancy. For emergency responders, the idea that if one person is not available another is designated to take that person's place is second nature. In schools, that is not so much the case. Even in daily operations, schools have a low level of redundancy. There is one person, the custodian, who knows how to open the loading dock—and no one else. There is one person, the main office administrative assistant, who has the password to the attendance system, or who knows how to replace the toner for the copier. Although this situation is inconvenient when the "keeper of the knowledge" is out sick, it's truly dangerous in emergency planning. If the only person who knows how to shut off the utilities, has training on the portable defibrillator, or can secure the gym is compromised or unavailable during the event—then what? As authority is decentralized and specific roles and responsibilities are designated as part of emergency planning, an appropriate level of redundancy needs to be incorporated. At least one or two other people must be able to perform the required operation or procedure.

So far, most of the examples from our work and experiences have been safety related. But the concept of redundancy is relevant beyond just safety concerns. Amy weighs in on this topic:

> When I was an elementary school principal, my son and daughter (twins!) were also students in my building. My son (who eventually became a first responder) considered himself the "assistant principal," and as such knew how to set up the projector and lower the screen in the gym for assemblies, movies, and so on (sounds dated, doesn't it?). It wasn't until two years later, on the first day of school, with a gym full of eager parents, teachers, and students, that I quickly discovered we lacked redundancy when it came to assemblies. Only my self-appointed "assistant principal" knew how to lower the screen or set up the projector—and he was now in the middle school across town! I ended up having to call his new school, get him out of class, and have him walk me through the procedure over the phone.

This is a funny and only slightly embarrassing example, but apply this idea to more high-stakes events such as turning off the gas after a boiler explosion or accessing the emergency medical forms following a bus accident on a field trip. Clearly, more than one person needs to know how to do the activities that are required in an emergency.

## High-Tech and Low-Tech Solutions

Another important consideration in emergency planning is to have redundancy in operational systems and protocols. Although the school's new software may be great for taking and maintaining attendance, do you have a means to account for students when there is no power or no cell tower service? Can you access medical records and emergency contact information for students when you are off site and away from a computer? We strongly recommend that redundancy of systems include both a high-tech and a low-tech solution for critical elements such as attendance, accountability, visitor sign-in, medical issues, and emergency contact information. Even if you have a great smartphone app that tells you which bus a student is on, you need access to a good old-fashioned paper version for the same information.

## Considerations for Training

School safety drills can only be effective and appropriate if they are conducted after all stakeholders have a solid foundation of training. Although many states require a school to have a certain number of drills per year, conducting an ineffective drill merely for the sake of compliance doesn't really make anyone safer. An exercise or drill should be done to ascertain the level of training and to test the plan along with those who will implement it, as part of a larger evaluative effort.

So, how do you train in a school? It's like eating an elephant—one bite at a time. First there needs to be a strong foundation of adequate, education-based training that is comprehensive and addresses all hazards—similar to the discussion we had in the EOP chapter. Unfortunately, active shooter training, although very popular, addresses one of the least likely crisis scenarios an educator will face. Yet an active shooter is the response that is most often practiced, in some cases because state law requires it. Often educators are provided with limited amounts of training that is very specific to an active shooter situation and are then expected to extrapolate this limited skill set into the myriad of potential crises that are likely to occur, from conflicts involving noncustodial parents to medical events to severe weather incidents.

The idea of training students often incites some active debate. The objections range from "it's too scary" to "you're training the next shooter." Let's unpack those ideas one at a time. Although the concern about scaring students may have some validity, this most often occurs when the training is not developmentally appropriate or grounded in best practices. The bitter reality is that students, regardless of their age, are well aware that violence occurs in schools and that there is the potential for violence in their school. Although the levels of concern and sophistication may vary from student to student, anxiety doesn't occur because students are trained about what to do in a lockdown, but rather because they *aren't* trained at all. What is even more anxiety-inducing to students than a potentially violent encounter at school is the appearance that there isn't a plan and no one knows what to do. When educators refuse to engage students in sensitive, appropriate discussions and trainings involving effective crisis response, they have planted the seeds or affirmed the idea that there isn't a plan and no one knows what to do to protect them.

In one of our trainings, a 1st grade teacher told us that the day after a school shooting occurred in a neighboring community, one of her students asked her, "What would you do if a bad guy came into our classroom?" Because her school had not adequately planned for safety or trained their staff and students, she was forced to give a vague answer about locking the door. She confided that her students essentially said, "That's it?" They looked equally dismayed, anxious, and horrified that they didn't know what to do, and apparently neither did the adults.

We often hear from well-meaning administrators that they don't want to train students because, based on research of past events, 80 percent of school shooters come from within the organization, either as current or former students or employees (Blair, Martaindale, & Nichols, 2014). These administrators believe that if they divulge details and procedures to students, the "next shooter" is encouraged to circumvent the emergency response. We strongly disagree with this contention. A student who is considering a shooting will be deterred, not encouraged, when a school has a high level of prevention, preparation, and training. The desired effect of a chaotic mass-casualty event where only the shooter is powerful and in control is dramatically altered when a specific plan is in place and every stakeholder is ready to actively respond.

Here are a number of other compelling reasons for students to be trained, active participants in drills and exercises:

- **The teacher will not always be there.** Although schools have a high level of adult supervision, students need to be able to respond appropriately without it. Students may find themselves alone in the restroom during a fire evacuation, or—in the unlikely but unthinkable possibility that many don't want to face—the teacher may go out into the hallway to investigate a suspicious noise and not come back as the shooting starts.
- **The skills required for students to effectively respond to a crisis event transfer to other areas.** Listening carefully and following directives is vital in a crisis event—and in becoming an effective learner. Making quick transitions from one activity or procedure to another assists in our crisis response—and is a good use of instructional time.
- **Knowing what to do in a crisis situation, and responding appropriately, is a life skill just as critical as any others taught in schools.** Our students encounter potential safety issues in their everyday lives outside of school—on mass transit, in shopping malls, or in their neighborhoods. They will someday go on to college and to workplaces, moving through a world that is rife with crisis events. Our students need to know how to keep themselves safe and how to respond to the threats they will inevitably encounter.

## Considerations for Drills and Exercises

When thinking about drilling and exercising the plan, it's important to think about what you're trying to accomplish. Consider the following questions:

- Is the point of the drill to examine potential vulnerabilities or problems with the response plan?

- Are you trying to provide an opportunity for stakeholders to practice or consider what to do in an emergency situation *without* the stress or "high stakes" of an actual event?
- Is the purpose to build capacity or "muscle memory" of how to respond in a stressful situation where reaction and training kick in rather than fear and panic?

We hope your answer is "yes" to all of these. What training and drills are *not* supposed to do is to test, panic, or intimidate untrained people. We sometimes see schools that want to make a drill "realistic," so they don't announce it as a drill, leaving students and staff to actually panic or they seek to make the crisis more intense by simulating gunshots or having a mock attacker. These ideas share at least two commonalities: (1) enormous liability is incurred when you pretend that there is an active shooter without *everyone* immediately knowing that it is a drill, and (2) creating unnecessary emotional trauma and panic solidifies the dangerous notion that no one knows what they are doing, intensifying the fear and perception of the school as a dangerous place. People who are untrained and don't know what to do already know that they are untrained and don't know what to do. There is no need for a drill to prove the point.

Some law enforcement officers (and even some school administrators) can be strong advocates of overly intense, realistic drills, based on their correct assumption that training and drills need to be frequent, ongoing, and appropriate to the situation. Unfortunately, this isn't often the case in education. The problem comes when you take a school full of people who have had little if any training and therefore have little foundational understanding of what they are trying to accomplish or how to accomplish it. The training they had most likely came from a law enforcement, not an education, perspective, so educators or students already feel intimidated and unsure. In other words, their training was infrequent, sporadic, and not appropriate to the unique needs of schools.

The most common drill that schools conduct is the good old-fashioned fire drill. The requirement for a monthly fire evacuation drill came about largely as a result of the Our Lady of the Angels fire that we discussed earlier. Schools have been conducting periodic fire drills for the last 50-plus years, so you would think that we would be really good at it, right? Wrong. Many of the problems associated with drills and exercises are illustrated by some of the common approaches to fire drills. As we review these, reflect on whether these same issues are true for the other response drills that are conducted at your school.

The first mistake made in drills is to plan, train, and practice for the drill rather than for the event itself. We have seen many response procedures that should have been about what to do when the building is on fire. Instead, they were about what to do in a fire drill—and that's an important distinction. If you are planning and training for the orderly movement of students on the same pre-ordained route to leave the building, then you are planning and training for a fire drill. When you are planning and training so that school stakeholders can effectively and strategically evacuate the building to escape a fire, that is a different matter.

In our reviews of emergency response procedures, we often see protocol titles like "Fire Drill Evacuation." These are often multistep plans that were designed for the convenience of the adults, and their end goal is to have an orderly evacuation of the building using one specific, designated route. When we change one variable (as would occur in an actual fire), such as blocking an exit or simulating missing students, the lack of preparedness for an actual fire, rather than a drill, becomes painfully clear. This planning pitfall was illustrated quite graphically in one middle school where we encountered a fire drill procedure that involved more than a dozen steps. This plan instructed that when the fire alarm goes off during the change of classes, students should proceed to their next-period class and then evacuate the building together as a class. Does this sound like an effective way to flee a burning building?

Effective drills and exercises should test the response procedure as you will most often find it—not when it is most convenient or least disruptive. Drills of all kinds should take place at nontraditional times, not just during class periods, but also at lunch, recess, or dismissal. You can't guarantee that you will only need to evacuate the school on sunny, warm days or when there aren't any substitutes or special schedules in place.

Although it may be less convenient and more disruptive, drills should mirror all the steps of the response. A tornado drill that requires students to just move into the general area of safety doesn't allow for an evaluation of whether they will all fit or whether they understand how (and why) to assume the recommended protective tornado position once they get there.

Conversely, educators sometimes attempt to apply traditional educational measures to crisis situations. In an emergency situation, students will not always be able to line up or wait for it to be quiet. The public address system will not always work, or the announcement may not be clear. There will not always be a designated "spot" for Mrs. Brown's class, or the classes may not arrive at the evacuation or shelter in perfect grade-level order.

Although logistics are important in drills, what is really critical is that staff and students do the following:

- Understand not just the response protocols but the rationale behind them.
- Think strategically about the general concepts of the procedure rather than cling doggedly to the minutiae when clearly they aren't working or applicable.
- View the drill as a practice for a potential event, rather than as a routine compliance exercise.
- Experience and be able to effectively respond to variables, inconveniences, and unexpected events in the drill itself.

We recommend that schools conduct periodic drills and practices of the response procedures for fires, severe weather events, and incidents of violence. The last of these, responding to active shooter events or other threats of violence, is often the most problematic.

So, what does an effective active shooter drill look like? Does it require simulated gunshots, intruders pounding on doors, students huddled in the corners crying? Or should a lockdown drill be a free-for-all during which teachers chat in the hallways while students hang out in the classroom socializing and taking lockdown selfies? (Yes, there is a hashtag, #lockdownselfies, which indicates how ridiculous and ineffective many lockdown drills are when done incorrectly. More alarmingly, many of the lockdown selfies are taken during lockdowns for actual events!)

An effective drill or exercise is a teaching activity. It is an opportunity for staff and students to stop their daily activities and focus on a specific response protocol with the aim of determining and implementing an appropriate reaction to the event. This can take many forms. Here's what an effective drill might look like:

- A school wants to practice a response to an active shooter event following the training of staff and students in evacuation and barricading response options as recommended by FEMA, DHS, and the Department of Education (see Chapter 6 for details).
- The principal gets on the PA system and says, "Attention, staff and students. We are now participating in an active shooter drill. Repeat: this is a drill." The principal goes on to provide specific communication that replicates what would be said in an actual active shooter situation—"We have an active shooter in the west gym"—and then stops. In classrooms, teachers lead a developmentally appropriate discussion with their students: "OK, the threat is in the west gym, and we are at the end of the east hallway. What would be our best option—evacuation or barricading?"
- Once the best option has been established—evacuation, for example—the teacher outlines how this would occur: how they would exit, where they would go, what problems may be encountered (crowding, running, etc.). The teacher then reframes the situation: "What if the threat is just down the hall? What would we do differently?" Then a discussion of barricading ensues. Depending on the time frame of the drill, the teacher might lead the students in a simulation of how they would barricade—what furniture would be used, what others should be doing—or may even have the class move outside via the evacuation route discussed.
- After a period of time, the principal announces that the drill has ended and an all-clear has been issued. The drill concludes with teachers answering questions, providing direction and clarification, and reassuring and reminding students of their roles in the response procedures.

In this drill, students were able to focus on the options they had to deal with the situation they faced, select an option, understand the reasoning behind the option chosen, and receive validation that there is a plan and they (and their teachers) know what to do. When drills consist of dramatic theatrics, apathetic compliance, or "party central," the critical practice of what to do is overshadowed and lost.

It's important to note here that this sample script can, and should, be used for a variety of drills, not just an active shooter situation. It would be equally effective when practicing other less dramatic but equally important response procedures.

## What About Parents?

The role of parents in training and drills should not be overlooked. We often see schools that create their emergency operations plans, drills, and trainings as though they had a school full of orphans. In a crisis event, parents will be an immediate and continual concern. Although some parents will overreact, interfere, and generally make our jobs more difficult (in more than just crisis events), educators must remember that all parents are sending us the thing that they value and protect quite literally more than anything else. With appropriate, ongoing communication and interaction, parents can be a valuable source of reinforcement, information, and support. Here are some suggestions for maximizing the role of parents in crisis training and drills.

### Keep Parents in the Loop

After a drill or training, students are going to go home and give their version of events. As a principal, it was always Amy's practice to get the correct version of events and information into the hands of parents before the students did. This was true when she gave a suspension, if the school's schedule had to be changed, or anytime something atypical occurred.

With today's notification systems, e-mail, and other communication capabilities, there is no reason for a parent to be uninformed about what safety training and drills are occurring. Almost every day there is a story in the media about a relatively low-level incident (e.g., an inappropriate social media posting or an altercation in the hallway) or even a training or drill in which administrators made the mistake of thinking that the parents would "never know" or "wouldn't care." Huge mistake! Without official communication from the school, parents resort to getting their misinformation about the event from group text messages, via social media, or on the bleachers at the volleyball game. A fairly innocuous incident or drill becomes embellished and twisted into a far greater threat than the reality, *and* parents become convinced that the school is refusing to tell them the truth about what is going on. Situations like these are avoidable. When the truth comes out, parents aren't upset about the thing that actually happened; the problem is the lack of communication.

## Teach Parents the Concepts, Vocabulary, and Rationale That You Are Using So That They Can Reinforce It at Home

We highly recommend that a common vocabulary be used throughout a school or district. Terms such as *leveled lockdown, barricading, reverse evacuation* (which we'll discuss in Chapter 6), and others need to be appropriately and consistently applied from staff to students and on to parents. It's confusing and often contradictory when parents are unaware of the meaning of certain terms or verbiage. Equally important is to make sure that parents are aware of what the response protocols are, and more significantly, what the rationale is behind them—meaning, how can these protocols keep their child safe? For assistance in this area, see *A Common Vocabulary for Crisis Response in Schools* located in the Resources section at www.eschool safety.org/resources.

When parents have multiple children in different grades across a given school district and both vocabulary and procedures are inconsistent, districts find themselves facing the perception of conflicting attitudes about school safety, whether it is justified or not. Inaccurate (or nonexistent) communication from school to home may lead a parent to believe that the high school has only one response procedure, that no one cares about safety in the middle school because they don't practice anything, and that the elementary principal has "gone rogue" and is expecting students to run away from a gunman. We see misapplication of terms all the time. For example, *shelter-in-place* becomes a response protocol for a chemical or biological incident, not a way to secure students from a potentially violent intruder. A Level 1 lockdown (when the threat is outside the building) becomes a *soft lockdown* or an *external lockdown* or a *restricted movement protocol*. All you're doing is putting different, confusing hats on a pig; it's still a pig.

## Talk Directly with Parents About Their Roles and Responsibilities in a Crisis Event

In previous chapters, we've discussed the need for response procedures that delineate what staff and students should do. In this chapter, we've also discussed how to train and practice so that school stakeholders can effectively respond. Be specific and explicit with parents about what you would ask them to do. This includes things like supporting the response procedures their children are taught, using appropriate means to get information about a crisis event (e.g., look at emergency communications such as a website or e-mails instead of calling the school), and developing family emergency plans with their children for early dismissals or other unexpected family or community emergencies.

It is a given that when a crisis event (or a rumor of a crisis event) occurs, parents *will* do something. Why not train and inform them so that "something" is beneficial and doesn't compromise the ability of responders to deal with the incident? A great example of this occurred in a high school we were working with. A student was sitting in the office waiting to see the principal and overheard a discussion between the assistant principal and the maintenance supervisor about an electrical panel that was smoking. What the student did not know was that the electrical panel was in the bus garage several blocks away and that the fire department was already on the scene. The student texted his mom that the school was most likely on fire and that the administration was not evacuating the building. In less than 15 minutes, a dozen parents were in the office wanting to know if their children were safe. If parents had been adequately trained and informed about what to do, they might have used other avenues of communication to get their information than the garbled text of a wayward student.

Practicing and living the plan, like the road to you-know-where, always begins with good intentions. Everyone understands that if you want someone to be able to do something effectively, you have to provide opportunities for instruction and remediation. It's a fundamental educational concept. Yet there is also a point at which the other daily demands of running a school or teaching a lesson take precedence (repeatedly) over practicing for an event that seems unlikely on a good day. The danger lies in the fact that without appropriate implementation and practice, even the best EOP becomes a document gathering dust on a shelf.

# Bringing
# Lockdown
# Up-to-Date

5

This chapter deals specifically with the most commonly implemented response procedure—lockdown—and the most commonly feared threat—a violent intruder. We provide an extensive examination of why traditional lockdown doesn't work and how it can be improved. We'll talk in depth about specific activities such as leveled lockdown, improving existing lockdown procedures, and developing lockdown enhancements and alternatives, with particular emphasis on the 2013 FEMA and Department of Education recommendations for a multiple-option, "run, hide, fight" approach to active shooter response in schools.

Whether it is justified or not, parents' worst fear when they send their child off to school is the threat of a school shooting. You can bet that the parents who answered the Gallup poll referenced in Chapter 1, in which parents indicated their level of fear for their child's safety, were thinking of an active shooter. As you will see in this chapter, although schools are in general one of the safest places for a child to be, violence can, and does, happen in even the "best," "safest" schools in the most "quintessentially American" towns. Furthermore, educators themselves fear the potential for violence in their schools and their perceived inability to adequately protect themselves and their students.

As an educational community, our response to these twin fears has been to cling to active shooter response procedures centered around a traditional lockdown that consists of locking the classroom door, hiding out in the classroom, and literally hoping for the best, despite overwhelming evidence and best-practice recommendations to the contrary. Quite simply, we can and must do better.

## Why Is Improvement Critical?

Just as no self-respecting teacher writes a lesson plan and then teaches the same unaltered lesson until retiring from the profession, deploying "traditional" lockdown procedures without any reflection, improvement, or knowledge of best practices in the field is unconscionable. Lockdown procedures originated in prisons to secure and protect inmates; however, after the mass shooting at Columbine High School, this secure-and-hold protocol began to be widely implemented in schools across the United States.

Traditional lockdowns in a school usually look like this: The teacher locks the door and turns off the lights while the students all huddle in one area. This protocol involves little more than holding still and hoping for the best.

The traditional lockdown approach is based on a number of dangerous assumptions that simply are not true. Let's examine the reality of past events and the academic research.

## What Do We Know from Past Events and Academic Research?

As human beings, we have a tendency to try to "make sense" of things by extrapolating our personal opinions or experiences and applying them to unsettling or unknown situations. Because school shootings are relatively rare yet extensively covered by the media, people tend to take their fragmented, isolated impressions and apply them to all school shooting events. If you went to your local grocery store and asked 10 people about school shootings, every person would have very specific opinions or perceptions, although very few of them would be accurate or grounded in the truth of past events. It is critical that an understanding of past active shooter events in schools be based upon what can be demonstrated to be true, not just what is "probably true." As you'll see in the upcoming section, many prevalent ideas about school shooting events are dangerously inaccurate.

Despite the surge of media attention in the last few years, violence has been present in public schools in the United States since their inception.

The statistical picture of violence in schools seems contradictory. On one hand, by many measures, our schools are becoming safer. For example, between 2001 and 2015, the percentage of 12- to 18-year-old students who reported victimization at school decreased overall from 6 percent to 3 percent. Students who reported theft decreased from 4 percent to 2 percent, and violent victimization went from 2 percent to 1 percent (McFarland et al., 2017). Other indicators of crime statistics in schools show a gradual decrease over time in rates of theft, assault, bullying, and sexual harassment (Zhang, Musu-Gillette, & Oudekerk, 2016).

On the other hand, in the last three years, there has been a dramatic increase in the rate of school-based bomb incidents, including bomb threats, the presence of explosive devices, and actual detonations (Klinger & Klinger, 2016). Perhaps most alarming is the accelerating increase in active shooter incidents in schools. From 2000 to 2006, there were an average of 6.4 active shooter events per year in schools. From 2007 to 2013, that rate had increased to 16.4 school shooting events per year (Blair & Schweit, 2014).

Looking more closely at active shooter incidents specifically in schools provokes a troubling revelation: Although school shootings are a relatively rare subset of potential crisis incidents, they are often mass-casualty events. Put another way, compared to other school violence, active shooter events don't happen that often; it is statistically unlikely that any given school will have an active shooter event. However, when a school shooting does happen, it is very often catastrophic. From 2000 to 2013, two of the four active shooter incidents with the highest casualty counts took place in a school (Blair & Schweit, 2014). This means that although preparing to respond to an active shooter cannot be the sole focus of any school safety plan, it is imperative that schools incorporate active shooter response protocols into their all-hazards emergency operations plans.

When we parse out just the active shooter incidents that have occurred specifically in educational settings over this same 13-year period, we find that 24.4 percent of shootings took place in schools, making schools the second most frequently attacked location, after workplaces (Blair & Schweit, 2014). Although 24.4 percent may not seem that high, it means almost one of every four shootings will take place in a school—and that speaks only to shooting events that meet the specific definition of an active shooter, which we will discuss later in this chapter. It does not incorporate other violent or potentially deadly attacks or incidents that also occur in schools.

Although only a quarter of all active shooter events took place in schools, a disproportionately large number of the highest-casualty events occurred in schools. As this book goes to press, the deadliest mass shootings in modern U.S. history were the Las Vegas shooting in 2017, with 58 fatalities; the Pulse nightclub shooting in Orlando in 2016, with 49 fatalities; Virginia Tech in 2007, with 32 killed; and Sandy Hook Elementary in 2012, with 26 fatalities.

There are many factors that make schools a "soft" target and contribute to the high number of injuries and fatalities in school-based active shooter events. Of these factors, the lack of training and the reliance on outdated, ineffective lockdown-response procedures are the most damaging (and the most preventable).

In 2013, FEMA, DHS, and the Department of Education issued recommendations about option-based lockdown procedures to be used when responding to an active shooter event. These protocols advocated rapid evacuation as the best option in this type of event. Despite these specific recommendations, in many schools today, the response procedure for an active shooter is to lock the door and keep the children out of sight. This approach generates a lot of problems, starting with the simple fact that most classroom doors have to be locked from the outside, have significant amounts of glass in them, and can be breached in literally seconds by a determined attacker. This "hide out and hope for the best" approach means that even when conditions exist for escaping a violent incident (such as the classroom having an exterior door or the attacker being at the far end of the building), students and staff are expected to passively sit in the danger zone and hope that the gunman doesn't make it to their location. Even worse, while waiting in the classroom for law enforcement to arrive and save the day, students are congregated together, making them easy targets if the gunman breaches the classroom.

## Debunking Common Lockdown Myths

Why do some schools continue to rely on an outdated response protocol that is no longer recommended by governmental agencies or experts in the field? A variety of possible reasons are applicable, including ignorance of the recommendation changes made in 2013, an unwillingness to invest the time and energy to make the necessary improvements, denial that the school will ever need to use an active shooter protocol, and a misguided belief that traditional lockdown "works just fine."

The stubborn belief that a traditional lockdown is effective is grounded in some dangerous inaccuracies, including the following:

- If you just hide out for a couple of minutes, law enforcement will come and save you.
- The locked door will keep a gunman out.
- If you keep quiet, a gunman will never know you're in here.
- If you run away, you will be shot.
- You can't have students running away from the school. How will you find them?

Before we unpack some of these inaccuracies and faulty assumptions, let's take a moment to explore some of the basic facts around some incidents. (The full reports for the tragedies discussed in this chapter are available in the Resources section at www.eschoolsafety.org/resources.)

## Columbine High School

One way to know that school lockdown procedures need to be refined is to look at past notable events. The 1999 massacre at Columbine High School in Jefferson County, Colorado, was a watershed moment in school safety. Twelve students and a teacher lost their lives that day in an event that unfolded on live TV in front of a horrified nation.

We know from after-incident reports that 10 students were killed in the library from 11:29 a.m. to 11:36 a.m. Just before this time, a Columbine teacher who was in the library placed one of many calls to 911. In the recording of the call, the teacher relays information to the dispatcher about their location and what the teacher thinks is happening, while gunshots and explosions can be heard in the background. Despite the proximity of an exterior exit through the back of the library, on several occasions the teacher instructs students to "get under the tables" or put their "heads under the tables." This teacher was instructing the students in a traditional lockdown protocol. Thankfully, not all students followed this protocol, and some instead evacuated the building to safety. We must not doubt the courage and actions of this teacher—she was simply doing what she had been trained and empowered to do. Sadly, 10 students died hiding under the tables in the library while undertaking a traditional lockdown protocol (Governors Columbine Review Commission, 2001).

Contrast the outcome in the library with what happened in other areas of the school. It is believed that roughly half of all Columbine students "self-evacuated," meaning they fled the building during the shooting without being trained or instructed to do so. The students who ignored the established secure-and-hold traditional lockdown procedure and instead self-evacuated survived the massacre.

### Virginia Tech

Not even 10 years later, the United States was once again struck with a horrific school tragedy, this time claiming the lives of 32 people at Virginia Tech in Blacksburg, Virginia. The governor's report of what happened that day shows the number of injuries, fatalities, and uninjured persons in each room of the second floor of Norris Hall, the site of the shooting itself (Virginia Tech Review Panel, 2007). In rooms 206, 211, and 207, it was reported that the occupants enacted a traditional lockdown protocol. Those rooms sustained extremely high rates of injuries and fatalities. Figure 5.1 shows that two rooms, 204 and 205, sustained far fewer casualties. In room 205, there were no injuries or fatalities (Virginia Tech Review Panel, 2007).

**FIGURE 5.1 |** Number of Injured, Fatalities, and Uninjured in Norris Hall, Virginia Tech

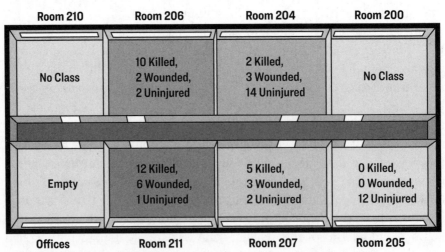

Source: © 2017 The Educator's School Safety Network.

How could the students in those rooms have fared so much better than their neighbors? The occupants of room 205 barricaded their room in addition to following the traditional lockdown procedures. They piled desks and chairs up against the door (despite its opening out into the hall) and were able to deny the shooter access to the room, although he tried to gain entry on five separate occasions (Virginia Tech Review Panel, 2007).

In room 204, a Holocaust survivor, Liviu Librescu, was teaching a class in solid mechanics. When the shooting began, he held the door shut just long enough for the majority of his students to escape out the windows. The injuries in room 204 were leg and ankle injuries sustained as students jumped from the second story. The fatalities in room 204 were Professor Librescu himself and a student who was unable or unwilling to make the jump (Virginia Tech Review Panel, 2007).

As was the case in Columbine, the occupants of rooms 204 and 205 who supplemented a traditional lockdown procedure by evacuating and barricading had not been trained or instructed to do so. Barricading and evacuating were not included in the official policy or procedure of Virginia Tech. On the absolute worst day, in terrifying conditions, the occupants of those rooms made their own decisions, and lives were saved as a result.

## Sandy Hook Elementary School

The myth that school violence occurs only at the secondary level was shattered on December 14, 2012, when 20 children and 6 adults were killed in a rampage shooting at Sandy Hook Elementary School in Newtown, Connecticut. Just as in the Columbine and Virginia Tech massacres, the gunman easily breached the classroom doors to gain access to and murder 1st grade students and staff who were hiding under desks or huddling in the back of the classroom. Just as in previous attacks, some students and staff who employed additional measures such as barricading doors or fleeing the scene survived. In one notable instance, a 1st grade student led eight of his classmates to safety as they rapidly evacuated after the shooter's weapon jammed (Sedensky, 2013). In previous incidents, high school and college-age students were actively engaged in going beyond a traditional lockdown to increase their chances of surviving the event. Events at Sandy Hook demonstrated that even very young students and elementary staff members were able to successfully deploy measures such as evacuation and barricading, all without having been trained or empowered to do so. Imagine how many lives could potentially be saved if all students and staff had the benefit of adequate, appropriate training in best-practice response measures for active shooter incidents.

## A Flawed Premise

As demonstrated in the incidents just described, a traditional response consisting of huddling quietly behind a locked door is based on the flawed premise that there isn't much we can do to save ourselves in an active shooting event, and if we hide out and wait for law enforcement, they will arrive in time to save the day. It has taken these tragic massacres to demonstrate that a passive, sit-and-wait approach is often a deadly mistake, and more important, that there *are* things we can do to increase our chances of surviving a violent event, such as barricading or fleeing the scene.

A 2014 study of the five highest-casualty active shooter events shows a median response time of three minutes (Blair & Schweit, 2014). Yet despite the best efforts and incredibly fast response time of law enforcement responders, they just cannot arrive fast enough. Between 2000 and 2013, 66.9 percent of all school shootings ended in less than five minutes, and 36 percent in less than two minutes, with 57 percent of all events resolved before police arrived (Blair & Schweit, 2014). (See Figure 5.2.)

The average length of a school shooting has shortened over time from an estimated 45 minutes for the 1999 shooting at Columbine High School to 87 seconds for the 2013 shooting at Arapahoe High School in suburban Denver. Even when a law enforcement official or school resource officer is on the scene and the response time is dramatically shortened, fatalities can occur—as was the case at Arapahoe, with two fatalities (Goodrum & Woodward, 2016).

At the Sandy Hook shooting, a 911 call was placed from the school within 4 minutes after the shooting began, yet Newtown police did not enter the building until almost 10 minutes later, a total of 14 minutes after the rampage began (Sedensky, 2013). During this short window of time, the shooter was able to inflict horrific damage despite law enforcement's best efforts to intervene.

It's not surprising, then, to note that most school shootings end violently, either with the shooter committing suicide or as a result of citizen,

**FIGURE 5.2 |** Timing Related to Active Shooter Incidents

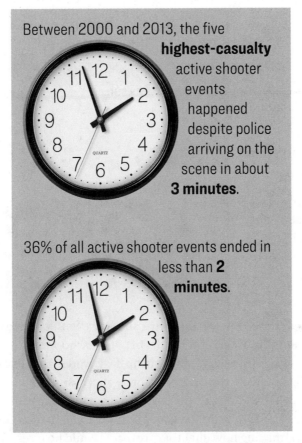

Between 2000 and 2013, the five **highest-casualty** active shooter events happened despite police arriving on the scene in about **3 minutes**.

36% of all active shooter events ended in less than **2 minutes**.

*Source:* Based on information in *A Study of Active Shooter Incidents, 2000–2013,* by J. Pete Blair and Katherine W. Schweit, 2014, Washington, DC: Texas State University and Federal Bureau of Investigation, U.S. Department of Justice.

not law enforcement, intervention. The tragic irony here is readily apparent. As shown in Figure 5.3, from 2000 to 2012, law enforcement officers with ongoing training and expertise in active shooter response were involved in the disposition of only about a third of all active shooter events in schools, whereas educators, who typically receive little to no training in crisis response, ended two-thirds of the attacks (NYPD Counterterrorism Bureau, 2012).

These lessons must be learned. It simply is not good enough that students attend schools across the United States and around the world where

**FIGURE 5.3** | Interventions in Active Shooter Incidents, 2000–2012

**2/3** **Non–law enforcement interventions**

80% are initiated by a single person.

**1/3**

**Law enforcement interventions**

70% are initiated by a solo officer.
30% are initiated by two or three officers.

the only option to respond to an active shooter event is a traditional lockdown. Looking at the successful results of people who simply did something other than holding still and hoping for the best, we see that lives depend on improving the standard procedures. Those successful results came about with absolutely no training or preparation. Imagine what educators could do to keep kids safe if they talked about options for active shooter response ahead of time. Imagine how effective protocols could be if response options were provided, and students and educators had developmentally appropriate (not scary) training to help them.

## Legal Questions

It's important to start any discussion of policy and legal questions by establishing a shared understanding of how the term *active shooter* is defined. The definition of an active shooter agreed upon by federal agencies such as the Department of Homeland Security, the FBI, FEMA, and the Department of Education is an individual who is actively "engaged in killing or attempting to kill people in a confined and populated area." Although this definition incorporates most of the school shootings of the past, it does not encompass potentially deadly situations in which an individual enters a school with a weapon and acts in a threatening fashion before actually beginning an attack. The protocols, practices, and approaches discussed in this chapter focus only on active shooter events and do not apply to other protocols and mandates that schools and districts may currently have in place.

As most educators know, new mandates and recommendations could always be around the corner. Any major shift in policy should give educators and administrators pause. Is the new policy within legal rights and duties? Can the school or district fulfill its critical obligation to do what is best for students while not opening itself to unnecessary legal liability? Conversely, will a reluctance or refusal to change or reexamine existing policies make a district even more vulnerable to legal action? Anytime a shift in policy or protocol occurs, the school's or the district's attorney should be contacted to ensure that the change fits within local, state, and federal laws.

Detractors of lockdown enhancements claim that straying from traditional lockdown unnecessarily exposes a school district to legal liability. This criticism is often poorly articulated and based on flimsy or nonexistent legal reasoning. Realistically, if a shooting occurs, the school district should *expect to be sued*. Dodging lawsuits or avoiding legal liability is *not* the goal of lockdown enhancements. The goal is to save lives, protect students and staff, and in doing so, minimize a school district's legal liability in potential lawsuits.

Despite no controlling legal precedent, it is fair to argue that employing a traditional lockdown protocol as the only option for active shooter response is a tenuous legal position. A court of law will not be moved by the argument that "we had a lockdown policy and executed it." According to general precedent regarding the negligence of schools, a defendant school is expected to uphold a reasonable "standard of care" of the students in its charge.

To determine the appropriate standard of care, a court would consider many sources for guidance. For instance, it would look to any federal or state recommendations of what is considered to be best practices for active shooter response. The court would also look to the lessons learned from previous school-based active shooter incidents to guide what a reasonable standard of care would be for a school's active shooter response.

Based on existing guidance, lessons learned, and what is widely considered to be best practice, it is difficult to imagine a situation in which a court would conclude that traditional lockdown alone is a reasonable standard of care for active shooter response. The recommendations from the federal Department of Education, the federal Department of Homeland Security, the New York Police Department active shooter report, and other recommendations from the International Association of Police Chiefs and other associations and authorities strongly indicate that a lockdown-only approach is no longer considered best practice. Additionally, looking at the results of school-based shootings and the fates of students in lockdown compared to those where other approaches were used leads to the conclusion that a lockdown-only approach is an inadequate standard of care.

In layperson's terms, the argument is fairly straightforward: If the recommendations of experts and government entities and established, research-based best practices indicate that a student has a better chance of surviving an active shooter event when lockdown enhancements such as evacuation and barricading are employed, how will a school district fare in front of a court if its defense consists of "We didn't want to change" or "We didn't know any better"?

Even more critical is the moral and ethical responsibility that educators have for the children in their care. If there are practices and procedures that are known to be more effective in keeping students safe, how can a school, a district, or an educator in good conscience refuse to implement these procedures because it seems "easier," "more convenient," or "more cost effective" to continue to cling to outdated, ineffective response protocols?

## How Can We Prevent Violence?

Strategic, effective violence prevention is one of the most critical (and underused) aspects of any organization's comprehensive all-hazards crisis planning and response. Although we have included discussions of some prevention activities throughout this book, there are so many strategies (and so many benefits) in a preventative approach to school safety that they simply cannot be covered adequately here. Nevertheless, they still demand your attention. As you evaluate, improve, and implement your school's crisis management capabilities, we encourage you to place violence-prevention measures high on your to-do list. With this in mind, we have

included an extensive selection of materials, research, and recommendations for violence prevention in the Resources section at www.eschool
safety.org/resources. If you check out only one of these supplemental sections, let it be this one.

## Improving Traditional Procedures with Leveled Lockdowns

At this point, it's critical to note that we are in no way saying that schools
should never use a traditional, "secure the kids" kind of lockdown. In
fact, in most instances it is appropriate to use a traditional lockdown. The
problem, as we have described, is relying on "traditional" lockdowns *alone*
during an active shooter event and neglecting to take other actions. There
is a critical need for an active, appropriate response to a life-or-death situation. The response to an active shooter–type event must be differentiated
from the response to more run-of-the-mill crisis incidents. The first step to
improve the effectiveness of traditional lockdown procedures is to implement a "leveled lockdown" approach.

Leveled lockdown is a means to differentiate the type, scope, and severity of a given incident. Let's examine four different potential crisis events
that could occur at a school:

- Someone robs the local carryout, and law enforcement is pursuing
  him through the neighborhood near the school.
- A staff member has a massive heart attack in the hallway outside the
  main office.
- A noncustodial parent becomes agitated in the office and heads
  upstairs to get his kid out of class.
- A disgruntled student pulls out a weapon in the cafeteria and starts
  shooting.

These events all require the enacting of a response protocol, yet each
requires a different level of response.

Leveled lockdown is a recommended best-practice protocol developed
by the U.S. Department of Education (U.S. Dept. of Education et al., 2013)
that allows schools to effectively differentiate among disparate events and
initiate an appropriate response from the classroom level on up. The chart
in Figure 5.4, which shows the essential points for lockdown Levels 1, 2,

and 3, is available as a full-size graphic (for use as a classroom sign) in the Resources section at www.eschoolsafety.org/resources.

**FIGURE 5.4 |** Lockdown Levels 1, 2, and 3

| Level 1 Lockdown | Level 2 Lockdown | Level 3 Lockdown |
|---|---|---|
| **The threat is outside the school.** | **The threat is inside the school.** | **Imminent, life-threatening danger—for example, an active shooter.** |
| • Exterior doors are locked and access into the school is restricted.<br>• Regular school day proceeds, with the exception that no one goes outside. | • Classrooms are locked.<br>• Students stay inside the classroom.<br>• School accounts for all students. | • Begin appropriate lockdown enhancements, such as barricading, rapid evacuation, and so on.<br>• If staying in classroom, barricade, turn off lights, stay quiet and out of sight. |

*Source:* © 2017 The Educator's School Safety Network.

## Level 1 Lockdown

A Level 1 lockdown is appropriate when the crisis event is outside of the school. This is the least severe and most frequently enacted type of lockdown. Although the crisis event has the potential to affect the school, presently the required response is to secure the school from the outside threat.

In a Level 1 lockdown, the following actions should be taken:

1. Secure the exterior doors of the school.
2. Restrict entry from outside.
3. Limit movement within the building.
4. Continue classes as usual.

Because the threat is outside the school, law enforcement typically initiates and concludes a Level 1 lockdown. Because such lockdowns are often lengthy in duration, it is advisable to follow normal school day routines as much as possible, within the noted restrictions. In classrooms, a Level 1 lockdown is not unlike business as usual. However, administrators, custodians, and support staff have additional duties securing the school and maintaining a higher than normal level of vigilance.

Even though the threat isn't happening inside the school, it is important to communicate information about the nature of the threat so that staff can respond appropriately. For example, if a school goes into a Level 1 lockdown because a person is fleeing from police, this information should be communicated to staff so they know to report a person running through the playground.

Although the recommendations for Level 1 are fairly straightforward, individual schools will need to address certain questions, such as the following:

- How will communication between areas of the school take place? Does the PA system reach all areas of the campus? If not, can radios be used to communicate to areas outside where students might be for class or recess? We have worked with schools that use an automated text message delivery system to alert staff. If a technological solution isn't feasible, schools can consider a system in which staff members are designated as "runners" to relay the information to areas that can't otherwise hear an announcement.
- What about students who have an early dismissal? Will Johnny's mom be allowed to pick him up for his dentist appointment? We have worked with schools that won't allow any entry or exit during any level of lockdown, which is the safest of all possible options, but as you might guess, parents are less than pleased when a "low-level" danger inconveniences them. As discussed throughout this book, schools need to strike a balance between reasonable safety precautions and the functioning of the school. A possible solution is a more rigorous screening of entry and exit during a Level 1 or Level 2 lockdown. A designated, trained person (such as a school resource officer or an administrator) meets and screens the person who is seeking to enter the building at the door before that person enters the building. Don't

forget, the staff in the building know you are in a leveled lockdown, but a person coming to deliver milk or fix the copier may not.

- In single or contiguous campus schools where students may move from one building to another throughout the school day, will they be allowed to go outside to do this? Typically, schools with multibuilding campuses will restrict student movement during a Level 1 or Level 2 lockdown. That restriction includes recess, field trips, outdoor band practice, the 8th graders who walk across the parking lot to the high school for algebra, and so on.

- How restricted will access to the school be? Can deliveries occur? Can buses drop off kids? These determinations should be made ahead of time, but most important, these expectations must be communicated, and those affected must be notified when a lockdown is enacted.

- What if this situation occurs at arrival or dismissal? Lockdowns at all levels should be practiced at nontraditional times, such as during lunch periods, arrival, and dismissal. Although it may not be convenient or easily done, schools must address the issue of how to notify, communicate, and move large groups of students during the unstructured, informal times that are part of the school day. A significant percentage of school shootings occur during these nonclassroom times, so dealing with this issue is crucial. The notion of securing 800 students who are in the gym for a pep rally is daunting. Administrators need to examine evacuation routes, options for sheltering, the ability to secure the gym, and other alternatives. Although the procedure may not be perfect and certainly won't be pretty, schools must plan and practice the capability to move and secure large groups of students, not just a classroom of 25.

- Will parents and other staff members be notified of the Level 1 lockdown? If so, how? Communicating with parents about emergency situations such as a lockdown is a double-edged sword. If parents are notified of the situation, they will typically react and act, often resulting in a flood of phone calls, a deluge of parents arriving at the building and complicating the response, and the inevitable criticisms about the way the situation was handled. Conversely, if parents are not told what is happening, the same things will still happen, just a bit later, with the added problem of mistrust and a guaranteed overreaction the next time a problem occurs. Add in the media attention and second-guessing, and a potentially small problem becomes a PR nightmare and a media bonanza. It is always best to communicate with parents as quickly and effectively as possible, providing general information about the nature of the event, the status and safety of the students, and instructions on what will be happening next. A crucial part of improving this potential no-win situation is to provide communication and training to parents *before* an event occurs. Without the emotion and stress of an actual event, parents can be briefed on what the lockdown procedures are, when these procedures will be enacted, what is being done to keep their child safe, and perhaps most important, what parents should do that will help, not hinder, the efforts of staff and emergency responders to deal with the situation.

## Level 2 Lockdown

A Level 2 lockdown occurs when the threat or problem, although not life threatening, is within the school. In a Level 2 lockdown, the following actions should be taken:

1. Classrooms are locked.
2. Students stay inside the classroom.
3. All students and staff are accounted for.
4. Instruction stops and classes do not change.
5. Students are moved out of the line of sight of the doors.
6. Staff members prepare to move to a Level 3, if needed.

Even though a Level 2 lockdown is not a life-or-death situation, it has the potential to become one. That noncustodial parent could produce a weapon or attack a staff member who stands in the way. In some Level 2 lockdowns, it's crucial that school stakeholders prepare themselves for the possibility that the event could escalate to a Level 3, life-or-death situation. This is a great example of why, in leveled lockdown, communication is critical. Staff members need to know the nature of the event in order to appropriately respond to it. If the point of the Level 2 lockdown is to keep students out of the halls and away from the medics working to save the stricken staff member's life, the likelihood is that the situation will not escalate in such a fashion as to affect each classroom.

Accounting for all students is a critical activity in a Level 2 lockdown. It sounds like such an easy task, yet even in a noncrisis event such as a field trip or a fire drill, schools often are not able to accurately account for the whereabouts of every student. Throughout a typical school day, students sign in and out, leave the classroom for the restroom, go to "specials" or other supplemental instruction areas, or are simply absent. In the chaos of a crisis event, information needs to be gathered quickly and efficiently as to the status of every student. Who is missing? Where are the missing students? Are they safe?

Schools need to develop systems by which the status and placement of all students, staff, and visitors can be determined with as much accuracy as possible. Many schools employ both low- and high-tech solutions to accountability, with individual classroom teachers taking attendance as the lockdown begins and relaying names of missing students to a centralized location via the public address system, e-mail, text messaging, telephone, or other means. It's important to designate and train a specific person to aggregate all this information. The main office staff may well have their hands full dealing with the crisis event. Other schools decide to have staff members report only if they have missing students. This cuts down on the amount of information to process but does not ensure that all staff members were able to account for their students.

Keep in mind that communication within the school needs to be objective and specific. Educators we have worked with or trained often hesitate at the thought of divulging information over the PA system, feeling that they will "tip off" the intruder or perpetrator. The shooter already knows he or she is the shooter—you aren't telling them anything they don't already know. When educators are pushing information out via the PA or phone system, they are providing valuable intelligence to those who are attempting to decide how to respond. Communicating that there is a noncustodial parent entering the 3rd grade hallway, for example, provides critical information to those who are attempting to shield students. Of course, you don't announce "Mrs. Smith is off her meds again and is trying to get her kid," but rather, "We have a noncustodial parent attempting to gain access to the 3rd grade wing."

In addition to the questions related to the Level 1 lockdown, Level 2 procedures raise questions that must be dealt with by each school or district:

- What is to be done about students who are not in a classroom when the lockdown begins? In a Level 2 lockdown, the threat is within the building, so it is critical that students not be stranded. Students need to understand that they must immediately move to a classroom or a safe area that can be secured and then notify someone of their presence rather than attempt to return to their classroom. Teachers should always do a quick "visual sweep" of the hallway outside as they secure their room and quickly bring in any students from the hallway and include them in their attendance check.

- What should students be doing in the classrooms during this time? Although a Level 3 lockdown requires students to react and move quickly, a Level 2 lockdown can be more of a waiting game. Just as staff members should be prepared if the situation escalates into a life-or-death situation, students should understand the need for them to be ready for further instructions or actions. This requires them to be calm, quiet, and under control. Teachers must maintain an appropriate balance between a "free time" social event and fearful panic by preparing students for what may happen next while providing reassurance that assistance is coming.

Similar concerns regarding unstructured nonclassroom times, communication within the building, and the notification of parents exist in Level 2 as in Level 1. Be sure to review the recommendations for the Level 1 lockdown through the lens of a more serious Level 2 lockdown situation.

## Level 3 Lockdown

In a Level 3 lockdown, schools must plan and prepare to take an active role in the response to an active shooter event. It is important to remember that a "run, hide, fight" type of lockdown is a last-resort option that is implemented in life-or-death situations. We are not advocating people running out of the building or barricading in classrooms when the issue is an unknown intruder wandering around the building stealing iPhones.

There is some concern that planning and preparing to take an active role in the response to an active shooter event is "beyond the scope" of the work of an educator. The old school of thought was that this type of work was best left to law enforcement officials, who have tactical and weapons training. However, our top law enforcement agency has recommended exactly the opposite. The FBI's study of active shooter incidents from 2000 to 2013 states: "Even when law enforcement was present or able to respond within minutes, *civilians often had to make life-and-death decisions*, and, therefore, *should be engaged in training* and discussions on decisions they may face" (Blair & Schweit, 2014, p. 8, emphasis added). It is not physically possible for law enforcement officials to be everywhere at all times, and in an active shooter event, there will be some delay (no matter how minimal) in law enforcement response. Once law enforcement does arrive on the scene, in the first few minutes, it may be only one officer who has to locate and move to the threat.

This critical time period is when civilian decision making is most critical —literally a matter of life and death. Planning and preparing to take an active role in active shooter response need not be the full-time job of an educator, and drills and planning must not be intimidating for adults or scary for students. This planning and preparation can and should be an empowering, measured, developmentally appropriate, commonsense approach that is part of a larger, all-hazards approach to school safety.

## The Three Tools of Level 3: Evacuation, Barricading, Countering

The "run, hide, fight" procedure is simply another way to designate the three tools of a Level 3 lockdown: evacuation, barricading, and countering (see Figure 5.5). Let's examine each of these more closely.

### Evacuation

Rapid evacuation is the first tool in the toolbox for a Level 3, life-or-death lockdown. Let's be clear here: in the context of a Level 3 lockdown, we are talking about a rapid, run-for-your-life evacuation, not an orderly "let's line up and leave the building" evacuation that you might use in the event of a fire alarm or a gas leak. A rapid evacuation is quite literally running for your life in an attempt to survive a potentially deadly event.

**FIGURE 5.5** | Three Basic Options

There are three basic options:
**run**, **hide**, or **fight**.
- You can **run away** from the shooter,
- seek a secure place where you can **hide** and/or deny the shooter access,
  or
- **incapacitate** the shooter to survive and protect others from harm . . .

*Source:* From *Guide for Developing High-Quality School Emergency Operations Plans* (p. 63), 2013, by U.S. Department of Education, Office of Elementary and Secondary Education, Office of Safe and Healthy Students, Washington, DC: Authors.

As shown in Figure 5.6, recommendations from FEMA, the Department of Homeland Security, and the U.S. Department of Education for active shooter response state that "if it is safe to do so for yourself and those in your care, the first course of action that should be taken is to run out of the building and far away until you are in a safe location" (U.S. Department of Education et al., 2013, p. 64).

**FIGURE 5.6** | Guideline for Evacuation

If it is safe to do so . . . the first course of action that should be taken is to run out of the building and far away until you are in a safe location.

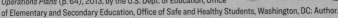

*Source:* From *Guide for Developing High-Quality School Emergency Operations Plans* (p. 64), 2013, by the U.S. Dept. of Education, Office of Elementary and Secondary Education, Office of Safe and Healthy Students, Washington, DC: Author.

Note that the recommendation places evacuation as the first, best option in an active shooter event. But this recommendation does not come without caveats. It is critical to also note that evacuation is the best option "when it is safe to do so." This raises some troubling questions—clearly the overall situation isn't "safe," as an active shooting event is occurring. That's why communication and information are so crucial. You need to know as much as possible about where the shooter is and what is happening. Sometimes, however, distance or facility-related factors make it safe to evacuate. If you have information that the event is happening in the main office in the west wing of the building and your classroom is in the east wing, evacuation is most likely a good, safe option rather than waiting in your classroom for the shooter to arrive in the east wing. If your classroom has an exterior exit door or windows on the first floor, evacuation can be a life-saving option even if the shooter is just down the hall.

So is it just a simple matter of running away at the first sign of trouble? Not necessarily. The first step in planning and training for a rapid evacuation is coming to an understanding of how to determine when evacuation is a safe option. Several elements are crucial in determining when and how to evacuate. These include considerations about the physical space: What are the assets and liabilities of the space? Every classroom or office has the potential for multiple evacuation exits—the doors and windows. Is there more than one door out of the classroom? Where does the door lead, and once out the door, what routes will you take to get out of the building? Are you on the first floor with large windows or an upper floor with limited options for climbing out the windows? The "upper-floor question" is particularly troubling. The specifics of the actual crisis event (such as proximity of the threat) and situational factors (such as the age of the students, the distance of the drop to the ground) must be taken into account and are unique to each classroom. In short, you will need to consider the lesser of two evils if you are forced into a life-or-death choice.

This determination of assets and liabilities in a given space is highly situational and subjective and is best accomplished with training and critical reflection before an active shooter event occurs (see the Resources section at www.eschoolsafety.org for more information). Teachers should critically analyze their particular classroom and school spaces to determine what their options are for evacuation. We highly recommend that staff members begin by physically walking around the school and locating all evacuation points—not just doors, but windows as well. Often teachers are unaware of where all the possible exits are and where some of the less traveled areas of the school lead to. After teachers have explored their evacuation options, they may want to lead their students on an "evacuation field trip," with the class walking through the building together so that students can learn where the various exits are and where they lead. It's important to include areas that are typically not accessible to students (such as the back door of the kitchen or the exit through the teachers lounge) to reinforce the notion that in a crisis event, these evacuation routes should be used. Teachers (and students) are creatures of habit and tend to use the same routes through the school every day. It's helpful for students to see other ways of exiting or moving through the building, such as taking a different hallway when going to music class, or leaving school at dismissal by using a different exit to the buses.

Another critical component in determining the likelihood of a safe evacuation is how to effectively disseminate the information about the nature of the violent event and where it is occurring. The closer you are to the event, the more critical it is to evacuate and do it quickly, yet the more likely it is that in your evacuation you will encounter the shooter. Communication about the event becomes very important here. If anyone witnessing the event has the capability to push out information with a description, location, and other critical information, you can quickly gauge where you are in relationship to the shooter's movements.

## Barricading

Barricading is a second survival tool that is particularly effective because it involves a low level of risk. Barricading is the practice of adding active steps to make the traditional lockdown protocol more effective. When barricading, teachers and students use furniture and other nearby objects to make it more difficult for the active shooter or other intruder to gain access to the barricaded area (see Figure 5.7). Because it is easy to implement as well as to undo, this approach can also be used in an escalating lockdown Level 2 situation or when the nature of the event is unclear. Whereas running away from the building or climbing out windows has some associated level of risk, simply moving the furniture in front of the classroom door has little to no risk, so barricading can be effectively used as a stopgap measure until the nature and severity of the crisis incident can be determined or until additional information is provided.

**FIGURE 5.7 |** Guideline for Barricading

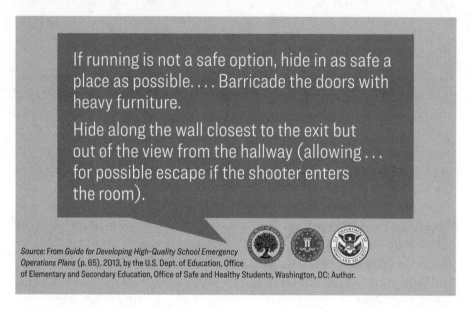

If running is not a safe option, hide in as safe a place as possible. . . . Barricade the doors with heavy furniture.

Hide along the wall closest to the exit but out of the view from the hallway (allowing . . . for possible escape if the shooter enters the room).

Source: From *Guide for Developing High-Quality School Emergency Operations Plans* (p. 65), 2013, by the U.S. Dept. of Education, Office of Elementary and Secondary Education, Office of Safe and Healthy Students, Washington, DC: Author.

When discussing barricading as a lockdown enhancement, people are quick to point out that classroom doors often open out into the hallway because of fire code restrictions. This does not preclude the use of barricading as an effective lockdown enhancement. The purpose of barricading is to delay and deter the active shooter, not create a fortified stronghold that can withstand attack for a full day. With a barricaded door, the shooter must first breach the lock, then get the door open, then remove the barricading items, all of which delay and impair the ability to inflict mass casualties. Keep in mind that 69 percent of active shooter events end in five minutes or less (Blair & Schweit, 2014). In more recent events, that time has been even shorter. Barricading the classroom door and delaying or denying the shooter access to the room accomplishes two important purposes: (1) It provides additional protection to those inside, and (2) a shooter occupied with trying to breach the barricade is not accomplishing the aim of killing people before law enforcement arrives on the scene.

Just as in evacuation, barricading raises questions and considerations. For example, not every stick of furniture needs to be shoved against the classroom door for barricading to be effective. It is critical to delay the intruder's access to the room, but it is equally important for those in the classroom to be able to remove the barricade and evacuate if the opportunity arises or other threats present themselves. In addition to denying access, barricades within the classroom itself (such as a table flipped over or filing cabinets pushed together) can provide a makeshift second line of defense for those in the room if the initial barricade is breached.

In the aftermath of school shooting tragedies, companies have rushed to develop "after market" devices that will secure the doors from inside. Although these devices work, they raise troubling issues. First, these devices, which are often quite costly, are designed to keep people safe in only one situation—that of an active shooter—and cannot be used effectively for anything else. Having to purchase one device for every classroom door can be cost-prohibitive; even more troubling, such purchases are using up resources that could have been expended to train staff and students to respond appropriately to all the potential crisis events a school is much more likely to face. In many states, these devices violate state fire or building codes as well, and they cannot be used after they are purchased by a well-intentioned district.

## Countering: A Last Resort

There is a reason why our discussion of the federal government's recommendations for "run, hide, fight" has focused almost exclusively on rapid evacuation and barricading. The Departments of Education and Homeland Security, along with FEMA, have provided very specific, pointed language as to the role of "fight," or countering, as a last resort when no other options remain (see Figure 5.8). They specify that countering should occur only "when confronted by the shooter," and that "adults in immediate danger should consider trying to . . . incapacitate the shooter by using aggressive force" (U.S. Department of Education et al., 2013, p. 65).

This is good advice for a variety of reasons. First and foremost, as discussed earlier, statistically speaking, most schools will not have an active shooter event. In the unlikely event that one does occur, the vast majority of students and staff will not come face to face with the shooter and should be using an evacuation and barricading response.

**FIGURE 5.8** | Guideline for Countering

If neither running nor hiding is a safe option, **as a last resort** when **confronted by the shooter**, adults in **immediate danger** should *consider* trying to disrupt or incapacitate the shooter by using aggressive force and items in their environment.

Source: From *Guide for Developing High-Quality School Emergency Operations Plans* (p. 65), 2013, by U.S. Dept. of Education, Office of Elementary and Secondary Education, Office of Safe and Healthy Students, Washington, DC: Author.

Unfortunately, the narrow focus of the federal government recommendation for countering (only adults should consider using force when encountering a shooter) is often lost in the zeal to attempt to protect children. For-profit entities, in addition to well-meaning individuals or organizations, often traumatize, intimidate, or overwhelm students and staff with training and discussions that focus on how to "fight" a gunman. This inappropriate emphasis on fighting a gunman typically comes at the expense of training time that could be better focused on understanding and internalizing the primary response options that people should be using: running away or barricading. When presented with the seemingly mundane notion of running away or moving furniture around, people (especially students) tend instead to focus on what may be either a quasi-exciting or absolutely terrifying idea of countering a deadly shooter. As a result, the concept that is most focused upon is the one that they are almost guaranteed not to need to use.

So let's take this a step further. Given these three options (run, hide, or fight) in training, one of which is highly stimulating and frightening, which one do you suppose students tell their parents about? Most likely their "training" to fight a gunman. When the media chooses to report on staff or student safety training in a school, which is the most interesting—and controversial—element? You guessed it—elementary school students fighting a gunman. Soon there are outraged parents, a media frenzy, and embattled administrators, and ultimately the board of education decides to forget the whole thing in the face of the storm. Now, instead of providing developmentally appropriate training for staff and students about effective ways to survive an active shooter event, districts revert back to the ineffective, but less controversial, traditional lockdown—"hide out and hope for the best."

Even if it were a good idea or a best-practice recommendation, training in fighting or countering has a high level of liability related to frequent injuries. As an example, Iowa saw such dramatic increases in workers compensation claims and lawsuits that its Homeland Security department discontinued funding these types of trainings (Dorn, January 2015). By May of 2015 in Iowa alone, more than $300,000 in emergency room bills had been paid to school employees injured in trainings that incorporated (and actively practiced) "fighting" a gunman (Dorn, May 13, 2015). Numerous lawsuits, either pending or settled out of court, have originated from injuries, accidents, and traumas resulting from creating a "realistic" active shooter event in a school, complete with unannounced drills, subduing mock gunmen, and discharging weapons outfitted with blanks. Is it truly worth the liability—creating a public relations nightmare and undermining the effectiveness of training —to include countering measures, at least in the little preparation that most educators and students receive? As an education-based training organization, we do not support the inclusion of a "fight" component in active shooter response training for staff and students.

## Essential Measures for All Lockdown Levels

Remember, the biggest concern about traditional lockdown practice is that it focuses on lockdowns *alone* and doesn't put enough emphasis on taking other critical actions. The more appropriate response is the leveled lockdown that we have described, but differentiating based on the level of the threat is only a first step. We encourage educators to maximize the effectiveness of the leveled lockdown by making the following practices the norm across all lockdown levels.

### Remove Distractors

Regardless of the level of lockdown, response protocols should be streamlined to the most essential components and presented in a prioritized fashion in a school's crisis plan or emergency operations plan, as covered in Chapter 3. The critical activities in Level 1 and 2 lockdowns are to secure the building and the students, account for everyone, and prepare to initiate additional activities as appropriate. Often well-meaning, overthinking strategists insert extraneous activities into the lockdown procedures that make them unnecessarily complicated at best, and force teachers to take their eyes off the prize—the safety of students—at worst. We often see lockdown drills in which teachers are frantically digging through a desk drawer to find the red or green cards that are intended to be used to signal the condition of the classroom occupants, agonizing over whether the curtains are supposed to be open or closed, or pawing through a bookcase to find the EOP plan instead of doing the critical activities of locking the door, securing the students, and accounting for who is missing.

We advise schools to work directly with their local emergency responders to determine whether additional activities such as closing curtains are effective, advantageous, or help with the response. If no one seems to understand the rationale behind such measures as closing the curtains or papering over the door windows, then perhaps you shouldn't be wasting response time doing them. The red and green cards in particular often seem to be used inappropriately. The intent is for a teacher to signal that someone in the room needs assistance by sliding a red card under the door and into the hallway, or using a green card to indicate that everyone within the room is OK. Although we agree with the underlying sentiment, we believe that signaling an active shooter as to which room is occupied or not is a terrible idea. These cards could be best put to use *after* the "all clear" has been given, to assist emergency responders in triaging which rooms to clear first.

## Work on Clear, Reliable Communication That Complies with Federal Requirements

Regardless of the response procedure being employed, clear, precise communication throughout the school is critical, and the use of "codes" only serves as an impediment to effective communication. In 2006 and again in 2009, the National Incident Management System (NIMS) issued a requirement that "plain language" be used for multiagency responses and recommended its use within single agencies, calling it "a matter of public safety" (Office of Emergency Communications, 2010, p. 5). Plain language (as defined by NIMS, DHS, and FEMA) eliminates the use of codes and acronyms as part of crisis response and replaces such codes and acronyms with common terminology.

Over the years, we have heard some incredibly creative codes. A school in rural Wyoming used the code "There is a bear in the swimming pool" to indicate a lockdown. A school in Louisiana used the code "The pink Cadillac in the parking lot has left its lights on," while an Ohio school would announce, "Please return the film *From Here to Eternity* to the office." (No, we are not making these up!) Although these examples are amusing, you might be able to imagine how bewildering and unhelpful these phrases would be in an actual emergency situation. Even simple color codes are problematic when, in a panic, a teacher is trying to remember whether "code orange" indicates an external threat or an active shooter. Without communication, staff will spend their time trying to determine what is happening instead of *responding* to what is happening.

Take care when adopting leveled lockdowns that the levels do not become codes themselves. When initiating a response procedure such as a Level 2 lockdown, it is not sufficient to simply announce "Level 2 lockdown." Instead, more specific information about the situation is necessary so that staff may respond appropriately. A better announcement might sound like this: "Attention, staff. We are going into a Level 2 lockdown because we have a noncustodial parent heading toward the 3rd grade hallway. Please secure classroom doors."

## Practice in Nontypical Situations

We often work with schools that are very self-satisfied with their capabilities to "lock down" their campus during class periods. They base their success on the ability to have every student secured in a locked room somewhere. This assumption suggests a couple of problems. Although you might be able to lock everyone up somewhere, can you account for all students, staff, and visitors during this time? More significantly, are you able to achieve this level of security in less structured times of the day, when, according to FEMA and our own research, an attack is much more likely? For example, does your lockdown procedure address securing 400 kids in the cafeteria, the large group of students congregating in the foyer before the first bell of the day, or the entire student body in the auditorium for an assembly? It is during these unstructured times that the school is much more vulnerable to attack and when traditional lockdown procedures are much more likely to be inadequate. We highly recommend practicing lockdowns before school, during lunches, at the change of classes, and during other nontraditional times and situations.

### Talk with Students and Staff About Rationale

It is vital to engage staff and students in their learning versus simply demanding compliance, as engagement yields much better results. Yet in school safety training, educators are often told what they must do without any explanation as to why a particular activity is important. It is not enough to simply issue edicts or orders, because unless people understand why it's important to do (or not do) something, the attitude toward compliance is going to be grudging at best. Remember our discussion in Chapter 1 about ID badges? Forcing compliance was ineffective, whereas engagement and understanding resulted in increased safety. The same is true with lockdown requirements. Students and staff need to know why it's important to account for everyone, to react to commands quickly, and to immediately obey commands from emergency responders.

### Improve Communications

Numerous reports and case studies after disasters such as Hurricane Katrina and the 9/11 attacks indicate that the greatest challenge in responding is not a lack of resources, staffing, or equipment, but communication. Schools are no different in this regard and must look beyond the typical modalities of communication that are used on a daily basis, such as PA systems or cell phones, and build a communication system that will work in a high-stress, chaotic situation where typical communication devices may not be available as a result of power outages, technological failures, or the physical inability to reach a given device. Often these systems already exist to some extent. We have seen numerous schools that have radios for communication both within a building and within a district, but no one carries them, they are not charged up, and there are no protocols for their use. Recent state and federal grants are available that provide radios and other tools for interagency communication systems, but often schools are not aware of, or are not involved in, the process for obtaining them.

Conversely, we have seen schools that thoughtfully and strategically purchased appropriate devices and systems, developed specific protocols for the use of this equipment daily as well as in a crisis, and trained their staff in both the mechanics of how to use the communication devices *and* the way in which they should be used. These successful organizations used the following devices and systems:

- Cell phones for group messaging and individual notification outside of the building infrastructure.
- Internal systems (such as phones, PA systems, and e-mail) for notification and accountability within the facility.
- Radios for communication between specific individuals as well as outside emergency responders.

## Include an Option for Autonomous Lockdown

In most schools, a lockdown (leveled or otherwise) is typically initiated from the office by the building principal regardless of where the crisis situation originated. Staff members often engage in an elaborate telephone game to relay information about the event to the office so that the principal can notify emergency responders and disseminate instructions to the rest of the staff. As a result, valuable time and accuracy of information are lost.

Every staff member should have the training and knowledge to initiate an autonomous lockdown from his or her location. This means that the person who first witnesses the intruder walking into the school with a weapon is the one who broadcasts to the school at large through the PA, phone, or other system about the location, nature, and severity of the incident in real time, saving precious minutes when people can begin to act to defend themselves from the threat. Once again, this recommendation comes not just from us, but from FEMA (2010).

We often get a bit of pushback on this recommendation in our trainings. Yes, we know your PA or telephone system doesn't currently have the capabilities to "all call" from every location, but typically this is a function that your provider can either enable or install with minimal, if any, costs. And despite administrators' apprehensions about potential staff overreaction or misuse of these systems, in our experience, we have not heard of staff with proper training and engagement making hysterical PA announcements for minor incidents such as a student tossing a chair or storming out of the classroom.

### Learn How to Call 911 Effectively

Given the prevalence and accessibility of 911 service, you would think that everyone knows how to respond to a crisis event using 911. Although even small children know how to call 911, most people need some training and guidance as to how to call 911 *effectively*. A few years ago we were training a staff of 140 teachers in a K–12 single-campus school. After our discussion about effective 911 calling, we took a break for lunch. Within 10 minutes the county sheriff burst into the school and approached us with an agitated question: "What are you guys doing?" As it turned out, after reflecting on how to call 911, most of the teachers were unsure of how it worked with their phone system and decided to give it a quick try before lunch. The sheriff's department had received more than 15 911 hang-up calls in less than 5 minutes. This story clearly illustrates two important points: (1) even if people say they know how to call 911, they are often not completely sure, and (2) in a crisis event you can call 911, drop the phone, and run out of the room—which, while not providing specific information, clearly will let emergency responders know that something is happening in the building.

It is also important to consider the issue of misusing 911. We have worked with schools where the teachers are not allowed to call 911 but must instead have someone in the office call. This approach compromises the critical information that emergency personnel need to respond to almost any crisis event, from an active shooter to a medical emergency. Dispatchers need to talk directly with the person witnessing the event so that person can relate the nature of the medical emergency, describe the intruder, or receive instructions about what to do. It can be a delicate balance—hesitating to call 911 and delaying the arrival of help, or provoking an unnecessarily intensive response for a low-level incident. Again, discussion and training with your local emergency responders will help to establish for staff the appropriate parameters for calling 911.

Although it is critical for staff to know how and when to call 911, it is equally important for them to make an additional call to the office so that the rest of the building knows what is happening and can either provide assistance or respond as the situation warrants. This can be accomplished by designating a second individual to contact the main office while the person speaking with 911 stays on the line with the emergency dispatcher.

In general, remember the following points:

- The person with "eyes on the event" is the one with whom the dispatcher wants to speak.
- The caller should give as much specific information as possible about the location and nature of the event.

We recommend putting specific location information directly on the phones themselves so that the caller can give clear information in the heat of the moment. For example, saying, "I'm in room 211, on the northwest corner of the A side of the building" is much clearer to responders who are most likely unfamiliar with the school than saying, "I'm in Mr. Murray's room at the end of the 6th grade hallway." Knowing the location of phones within the room is also critical. Try it sometime—walk into an unfamiliar classroom and attempt to find the phone within five seconds. Chances are the phone is in a different place in each classroom—sometimes on a desk, sometimes on a wall, sometimes hidden underneath ungraded papers or student artwork. Classroom phones should be clearly visible and consistently placed in classrooms throughout the school.

## Final Thoughts

Educators often wonder whether they've considered all the critical aspects of an effective active shooter response. In many cases, the lockdown procedures for any type of event need to be improved. If you want to critically evaluate the effectiveness of your school's active shooter or lockdown protocols, consider taking the *Is Our Response Effective?* self-assessment, available in the Resources section www.eschoolsafety.org.

The notion of responding appropriately and effectively to a crisis event—specifically using a lockdown or enhanced lockdown protocol—can seem overwhelming at best. For every situation or recommendation we've discussed in this chapter, you can most likely think of a "what if" scenario that is in opposition to the best-practice recommendations. Often this sense of confusion, along with the seemingly innumerable possible crisis events, causes educators to feel that their efforts are futile.

Nothing could be further from the truth. The only thing that you can do to make the situation worse, or to make your school more unsafe, is to do nothing. Any measures, no matter how small, taken in a thoughtful manner that are based on best-practice recommendations, are better than refusing to deal with the issue and doing nothing just to keep from doing something wrong. The Educator's School Safety Network provides training in lockdown enhancements and active shooter response that is available in a variety of formats. For more information, see the Training section at www. eschoolsafety.org.

In this chapter, we began by demonstrating how individuals with no training or authority to do so were able to increase their chances of surviving a tragedy and save the lives of others. Imagine the impact that training and planning for crisis events can have in your school.

# It's Not Just About Lockdown: Other Necessary Response Procedures

After the detailed examination of active shooter response and lockdown in the previous chapter, we will now focus on the other response procedures suggested by FEMA and the U.S. Department of Homeland Security, as they are more likely to be implemented in a given school. These response procedures are evacuation; reverse evacuation; shelter-in-place; drop, cover, and hold; and responding to a bomb incident. We'll look at these procedures both in terms of the suggested response activities as well as specific issues that school decision makers will need to address.

## Thinking in Terms of Response, Not Incident

When we conduct vulnerability assessments, we look at the flip charts or emergency operations information that teachers keep close at hand. The flip charts typically have a page for each common incident or hazard, and then detailed written procedures for how employees should respond. This method of organization presents a few problems:

- It gives the false impression that a school has 10 different responses for 10 different incidents.
- It requires EOP team members to come up with all possible hypothetical hazards so that they can all be listed and a response procedure can be solidified.
- It falsely concludes that when A happens, you will always respond with B. For example, if a flash flood causes part of the school to collapse in a sinkhole, then evacuating the school is necessary. However, if the flood causes the athletic fields and outlying areas of the school to be unsafe but the school building itself is on high ground, reverse evacuation is appropriate.

The flip charts in many schools also present logistical and organizational problems. In some buildings we see several versions of flip charts (often with contradictory or outdated information) that are located in various places in a classroom (such as hidden in a drawer, buried under a pile of papers, stuck in a bookshelf, or tacked to the wall). A well-written, helpful flip chart is useless if no one can find it in a panic situation, or if, when it is found, it is incorrect.

In reality, no matter how many combinations of threats a creative EOP planning team can imagine, schools really use only slightly modified versions of the standard response procedures we mentioned at the start of this chapter: evacuation; reverse evacuation; shelter-in-place; drop, cover, and hold; and lockdown. If you have to evacuate the school because there is a fire, the response procedure isn't fundamentally different than if you have to evacuate for a gas leak or a building collapse. The intent in all these possibilities is to evacuate people and move them away from danger toward safety.

This shift in thinking not only simplifies flip charts and EOPs but also makes emergency response seem less overwhelming and more manageable. With training in how to master these five skills (standard response procedures), staff can feel empowered to assess the situation and choose the response that is most appropriate.

## Standard Response Procedures

Let's begin with a discussion of each of the standard response procedures, framed by the following questions: What does this procedure accomplish?

When might I commonly use it? What special considerations should I keep in mind?

## Evacuation

**What does this procedure accomplish?** Evacuation consists simply of moving people from a danger inside a building to safety outside. Evacuation is appropriate any time the school building is unsafe and the outdoors (or other evacuation site) is comparatively safer. It is important to distinguish between a standard evacuation and a rapid evacuation. Standard evacuation is initiated by a command, executed in an organized fashion, and led by teachers or staff. As discussed in the previous chapter, rapid evacuation is only appropriate in life-or-death situations, is not always initiated by a command, is most likely chaotic and disorganized, and may involve students running for their lives without a teacher or staff member. In either case (standard or rapid), evacuation requires planning and training before implementation and at some point (either during or after) demands accountability of staff and students.

**When might I commonly use it?** Evacuation is most commonly used in the event of a fire, a gas leak, an explosion, or any structural issue with the building that makes it unsafe to occupy. Sometimes the evacuation protocol is used in conjunction with other protocols when responding to an incident. For example, a school enacts the "drop, cover, and hold" protocol in response to an earthquake, which damages the building, which makes it structurally unsafe, which requires evacuating to safety.

**What special considerations should I keep in mind?** After reaching safety outdoors or at an evacuation site, the most important consideration for evacuation is the need to account for students, staff, and anyone else who was in the building as it was evacuated. When planning for accounting for students, be sure to consider these questions: Are class rosters up to date? If the procedure is to access student attendance information online, is there a plan for bringing laptops, tablets, or phones? Are chargers or other power sources needed for those devices? What if there is no Wi-Fi or a grid failure knocks out cell phone reception? Is there a low-tech backup solution? Is there a system in place before the crisis event to ensure that paper records are up-to-date?

Accounting for visitors, substitutes, or itinerant staff is a challenge. An easy solution is to keep accurate sign-in sheets of who enters and exits the building and to take those logs along when the building is evacuated. (This practice has the added benefit of providing a satisfactory explanation for those who bristle at having to sign in. "If we have to evacuate this building for an emergency, would you like us to be able to account for you? If so, please sign in.")

Schools should have at least one evacuation site, although it is preferable they have two. Check the evacuation route. Will students need to cross busy streets? Is it possible to sweep the evacuation route for dangers? Having several evacuation sites is helpful not only for redundancy but also to deter violence. If an attacker's plan is to call a threat in to the school and then place explosive devices at the evacuation site, having multiple possible evacuation sites and not choosing an option until evacuation commences keeps a would-be attacker in the dark.

We have worked with school districts that found it helpful to create a separate page on the district website with helpful information for each possible evacuation site. The pages are hidden until there is actual need for evacuation, at which point they are activated so that parents can see information about parent reunification, including where to park and how to pick up their students. Some school districts have a "safety" page that is always active and provides general information about safety activities and protocols in the district. (Keep in mind that this page should not make detailed, specific information available to a would-be attacker, but rather provide a general overview of the planning and preparedness that has taken place in the district. The knowledge that the district has anticipated and planned for events is most likely a deterrent.) Then there are specific emergency pages that can be deployed, depending on the nature of the crisis event, that provide instructions and information to school stakeholders.

## Reverse Evacuation

**What does this procedure accomplish?** Reverse evacuation involves bringing people from the danger or threat that exists outdoors to relative safety inside the school building.

**When might I commonly use it?** Reverse evacuation is appropriate anytime that it becomes unsafe to remain outdoors. The most typical use is when severe weather threatens; however, reverse evacuation is appropriate if there is another danger in the vicinity of the school, such as police activity, unusual utility work, crowds, or a traffic accident.

**What special considerations should I keep in mind?** The most important (and potentially overlooked) consideration for reverse evacuation is communication. Can the staff members outside easily communicate with those indoors? Are two-way radios available? Does anyone in the office know when a group is outside? More important, does someone take and use a radio each time he or she is outside? Does the PA system reach outdoor areas where students may be?

Communication protocols for evacuation (and reverse evacuation) should be clearly established, in particular when there are daily recess periods, physical education classes, and athletic practices that occur outside. We have seen several instances in which a violent event occurred in the school, but because communication protocols were absent, students who were outside (out of reach of the event) were unwittingly brought back into the area of danger. In one memorable case, the school enacted its severe weather response when a tornado warning was issued, but poor communication meant that the outside PE class was not notified until several minutes later.

It is relatively easy to implement good communication practices for routine outdoor activities such as recess or PE class, but what about the spontaneous use of the outdoors? If a teacher lets students read outside on a nice summer day, is there a means by which the office can communicate with the class if the school is notified that law enforcement is serving a warrant down the street?

In general, adults who are supervising students outside should always have a mechanism by which they can both receive and initiate communication. This could be a radio (at best) or a cell phone (at least), but these tools alone are not enough. There needs to be an established daily protocol for two-way communication that is not limited to just crisis events. This serves to make communication with those outside of the facility a standard operating procedure.

### Shelter-in-Place

Shelter-in-place is the very specific response to a chemical, biological, radiological, nuclear, or explosive (CBRNE) event. Although shelter-in-place is sometimes erroneously used interchangeably with lockdown, shelter-in-place should be used only in response to a CBRNE event.

**What does this procedure accomplish?** Shelter-in-place procedures seal off the school building (as appropriate) to shield people from the harmful fumes, radiation, powders, dusts, or other materials related to a CBRNE event. When sheltering in place, doors and windows are closed and locked and in some cases may be sealed with plastic, wet towels, or other materials. Heating, ventilation, and air conditioning (HVAC) systems should be shut down. Emergency responders will most likely provide specific directions to the school (such as moving people to a lower floor or other activities), based on the nature of the event, weather conditions, and other factors. When sheltering in place, whoever is in the school stays there, and no one may enter during the event.

**When might I commonly use it?** Shelter-in-place may be used if there is an attack that involves CBRNE weapons, or a chemical spill or other accident. Be sure to consider your school's proximity to industrial areas, train lines, highways, or other potential sites for such accidents or spills. Although all schools should have this response procedure in place, for some facilities it is more of a priority. Check with your local emergency responders to see what type of events they are training for. We are often surprised to learn that schools within just a few miles of highways or railways that carry potentially hazardous materials have never worked with local responders to determine the level of threat or the recommended responses. A quick view of your school on Google Earth will illustrate how close you are to industrial sites, airports, or transportation hubs that may create vulnerabilities for the school.

**What special considerations should I keep in mind?** Communication with parents is critical. The building may not be unsealed and parents may not have access to their children until emergency responders have deemed it safe to do so. If possible, allow students with phones to contact parents indicating they are safe but will have to remain in the school until parent reunification begins. A specific web page, to be activated in the unlikely event of sheltering-in-place, can be helpful to direct parent inquiries, as there will be many, and phone lines need to be kept clear for emergency communication with law enforcement and other first responders.

If possible, consider sheltering in a windowless room on the first floor of a building away from exposure to wind and air circulation, but not the basement. Many chemicals are heavier than air and can seep into a basement, even if it is sealed. Your local first responders will have specific information and response recommendations that are based on the unique vulnerabilities of your area, so their input is vital.

Be sure that you have identified individuals who know how to shut off and seal HVAC systems. Many schools have air handlers that automatically circulate air from the outside into the school. All such systems *must* be turned off and sealed when sheltering in place. If only one person knows how to do so, be sure to train at least two more people so there is redundancy. When we conduct vulnerability assessments, we always ask which individuals know how to turn off the utilities to the building *and* if they are present in the building at that moment. The majority of time there is only a single maintenance person who knows how to complete this critical task. Fortunately, it usually takes just a matter of minutes to show members of the administrative and custodial staffs what to do, so this is an easy fix.

### Drop, Cover, and Hold

**What does this procedure accomplish?** Dropping to the floor and seeking cover under desks and tables provides safety from falling objects and debris when there isn't enough time to move people to shelter.

**When might I commonly use it?** Drop, cover, and hold is most commonly used as an earthquake response but may be used anytime an accident, an explosion, or a sudden weather event causes objects and debris to fall. For example, if a windstorm damages the roof suddenly, it is appropriate to drop, cover, and hold until the initial damage is done and the building can be evacuated.

**What special considerations should I keep in mind?** Talk with students ahead of time about drop, cover, and hold. When it is necessary to enact this procedure, there will be no time to discuss the rationale or to reassure or cajole students. Drop, cover, and hold is what we call a "lightning command"—one that must be immediately obeyed without delay or discussion. This explanation need not be scary and must be developmentally appropriate. The skill of quickly executing certain commands can be practiced in nonemergency situations, but the ability to quickly follow directives without debate is an important safety skill for students.

We've seen teachers at all grade levels employ lightning commands with success that extends beyond just safety concerns. For example, one teacher uses an "eyes on me" command that consists of students immediately "freezing," becoming silent, and looking directly at the teacher. Although it took some practice and training, this teacher is able to use this command when she needs students' immediate attention for a change in plans, clarification on directions, or in a safety context, when she needs them to rapidly evacuate the classroom or dive under their desks. Like any technique, overuse or overreliance dulls the effect.

## After-Hours Responses

With any response procedure, be sure to determine if there is a plan and communications process in place to respond after hours. Who is the incident commander when the administrator isn't in the building? What are the procedures for building and sitewide communication after hours?

One of the most frightening and potentially devastating issues that we consistently see in our work with schools is a complete lack of planning and training for crisis events that occur after school has dismissed. More and more, schools are being used for child care, community events, athletic contests, and various other activities both before and after traditional school hours. At the same time, rarely are there adequate response procedures and people who are trained to use them during these critical times. Does anyone legitimately believe that fires, floods, accidents, or active shooter events will conveniently occur only between 8 a.m. and 3 p.m.?

Next time you have an evening with nothing else to do (OK, we know that doesn't happen), drop into a school around dinner time. This is what you might find. The building is still unlocked, so you have access to the public areas. There is no one around who is "in charge," yet there are some practices, rehearsals, or meetings happening. A few overwhelmed teachers are finishing up in classrooms, while the custodial staff is cleaning somewhere. A handful of randomly unsupervised students or siblings are running around or sitting somewhere, focused on their phones. Now imagine that you hear shots fired somewhere in the building, or a wildfire is rushing toward the facility, or a car has crashed into the gym lobby. Who's in charge? Who's making decisions? What communication systems are in place? How do you know who is actually in the building and must be saved or accounted for? Most important, have the individuals who are still in the building (coaches, custodians, afterschool child care providers) been trained in what to do? Most likely they have not. The result may well be chaos and casualties.

The vulnerabilities of a school in this situation were graphically illustrated to us one fall evening during an after-hours check at a large high school where we were doing a vulnerability assessment. The weather was unsettled, and a tornado watch had been issued in anticipation of more severe weather to follow. The school had about a hundred people in the gym watching a volleyball game, 30 or more parents in the library for a PTO meeting, and a group of students in the auditorium rehearsing for the fall play. We struggled to find anyone "in charge" and finally asked the custodian what would happen if the anticipated severe weather materialized. She replied that she would call the superintendent and see "what he wanted to do." (Perhaps the superintendent would cancel the tornado?) A few more questions determined that this was not a great plan for several reasons: (1) the custodian did not have access to a weather radio or any other means to know if severe weather was imminent; (2) she didn't have a phone to call the superintendent; (3) she didn't have the superintendent's phone number; (4) she was unaware of any response protocols for severe weather; and (5) she didn't know how to use the PA or any other system to communicate with the building at large. We'll let you fill in the blanks on how well this "plan" was going to work.

We have also worked with schools that have taken their formalized response procedures and strategically applied them to before- and after-hours situations. They created protocols that addressed the many variables that occur outside the traditional school day and provided a framework for adequate preparation and response to potential crisis events. These organizations ensured that the necessary equipment, personnel, and—most important—training were allocated to the critically vulnerable times before and after school. Staff members such as coaches, custodians, supervisors, club advisors, and others present in the building were given specific response tasks and trained in how to accomplish them.

Information and suggestions for assessing and mitigating after-hours issues are available in the Resource section at www.eschoolsafety.org/resources. The Educator's School Safety Network also provides training for after-hours preparedness and crisis response.

## Special Considerations for Bomb Threats and Incidents

Bomb incidents in schools has been an area of particular interest and concern for us over the past few years. It began when we started to see an increasing number of schools caught in a destructive cycle of (1) bomb threat, (2) response/disruption, and (3) upset students and parents—repeated over and over, at great cost financially as well as in terms of public relations and instruction. After finding that there was no central clearinghouse agency that tracked bomb incidents and violent threats in schools, our organization began to aggregate data to determine the scope and severity of the problem. Our ongoing research indicates that school-based bomb threats and incidents are a widespread problem that most educators haven't received any training or tools to address. (Past and current *Bomb Incidents in Schools* reports are available in the Resources section at www.eschoolsafety.org). More alarmingly, once a school receives an initial bomb threat, it (or schools in the immediate vicinity) is much more likely to experience several more. (There was a period of several weeks during the 2015–2016 school year when several schools in Guam were evacuating two or three times per day because of multiple bomb threats.) The situation is frustrating because the problems and costs associated with bomb threats could be effectively mitigated if appropriate training and response protocols were implemented.

As we discussed in Chapter 1, the past several years have seen a dramatic increase in school-related bomb incidents both in the United States and throughout the world. It's also important to note that these are not just empty threats. In recent years, officials have made startling discoveries of bomb-making materials in the possession of students with legitimate plans for a school attack. In fact, data from the Bureau of Alcohol, Tobacco, Firearms, and Explosives indicate that juvenile bomb makers have a higher success rate of detonations than the national average (Newman, 2011). Between January 1990 and February 2002, there were 1,055 incidents of bombs being placed on school premises (Bureau of Alcohol, Tobacco, Firearms, and Explosives, 2003). Our research indicates that there are multiple incidents in which explosive devices are either found or detonated every school year. It is troubling to note that four explosive devices were found and one detonation occurred in U.S. schools in the 2015–2016 school year alone; in 2016, four detonations occurred just in August (Klinger & Klinger, 2017). Even more alarming are data provided to us from the U.S. Bomb Data

Center of the Bureau of Alcohol, Tobacco, Firearms, and Explosives, which indicate 120 instances of explosive devices or detonations in schools from 2012 to 2016.

One of the most problematic issues associated with bomb threats is the misconception that all the school has to do is call law enforcement, which will come in, find the culprit, and decide exactly what to do. Unfortunately, although first responders will collaborate with and assist school leaders, the appropriate procedure, as noted in Figure 6.1, is that "organizational, on-site decision makers should determine evacuation" (Energetic Materials Research and Testing Center, 2010). This means school leaders will be faced with the daunting tasks of finding the threat, evaluating the validity of the threat, determining whether to evacuate or not, implementing the chosen response protocol, conducting or assisting in an investigation to find the perpetrator of the threat, and then dealing with the public relations fallout regarding any of the five previous decisions we just listed. And did we mention that all of these activities could occur without a bit of training?

**FIGURE 6.1** | Guidelines for Evacuation Decisions

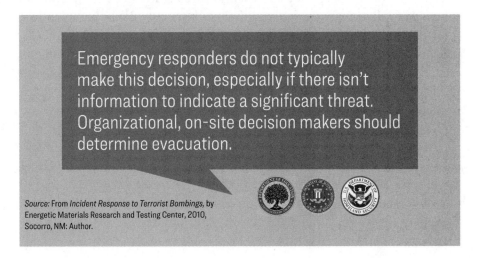

Emergency responders do not typically make this decision, especially if there isn't information to indicate a significant threat. Organizational, on-site decision makers should determine evacuation.

*Source:* From *Incident Response to Terrorist Bombings,* by Energetic Materials Research and Testing Center, 2010, Socorro, NM: Author.

Keep in mind that all of this is predicated on the assumption that the incident is only a threat. In reality, schools must also be prepared to deal with potential explosives such as suspicious packages, as well as actual detonations. This level of preparedness calls for a robust, well-thought-out protocol for bomb incidents that covers threats, potential explosives, and post-detonation response.

## Types of Threats and Perpetrators

Bomb threats come in all shapes and sizes and are perpetrated by a wide variety of individuals in an array of settings. The threats range from simply a misspelled "boomb threat" scrawled on a bathroom stall to an 18-year-old in Israel who advertised on the "dark web" marketplace, charging $30 in Bitcoin to threaten schools—and was hired to do so more than 200 times (Green, 2017). This reality makes it difficult—and potentially dangerous— to generalize about what the threat will be like and what should be done. Our research indicates a number of disturbing trends. Contrary to popular belief, most bomb threats are not made by phone. A significant number are received in schools via e-mail, social media, and in person through verbal threats made by students or angry rants from an enraged parent. In the majority of cases, but not all, the threat is found within the school, most often as a note or drawing discovered in a restroom (Klinger & Klinger, 2017). Most of the perpetrators of bomb threats are students within the school, but a disquieting number are people from outside the organization, including students from other schools, disgruntled community members, parents, or employees, as well as internet-based "swatters" who employ simultaneous, geographically diverse threats to enjoy the chaos that ensues (Klinger & Klinger, 2017). Although a majority of bomb threats take place in secondary settings (high schools in particular), elementary schools are targeted frequently as well, typically by adults outside of the organization.

It is dangerous to assume that the bomb threat will be "just" a threat— called in by a high school student to his or her own school as a means to get out of class. It is just as likely that a district will need to effectively respond to a secondhand social media posting from an adult in another state alleging that explosives have been planted on the grounds of one of their five elementary schools.

## Evaluating a Bomb Threat

The constraints of this book mean that it cannot adequately train anyone to effectively evaluate bomb threats; however, as with other threats of violence, examining the characteristics of the threat and other related evidence can provide insight as to the validity of the threat and how to respond to it. In general, the more specific the threat, the greater the level of risk. A note scrawled on the bathroom stall that says "Boom" is less of a threat than the social media post that specifies a time, date, and location (e.g., "By the end of the day today, Eisenhower High School gets what it deserves when the stadium goes boom!").

Specificity is believed to be the best guide as to how serious the threat is and is usually indicated by the following factors:

- Place and time indicated in the threat.
- Description of the bomb to be used.
- Specific targets mentioned or indicated.
- Reason given or implied in the threat.

It bears repeating: In general, more specific details generally indicate a more credible threat.

### Responding to a Bomb Threat

The most common response to a bomb threat is to evacuate the school using the evacuation response protocol we discussed earlier in this chapter. This is not always the safest or best alternative and should not be an automatic "default" position for the following reasons:

- You may be taking students from the relative safety of a secured school building out into a larger threat area, as the selected evacuation site may itself present significant vulnerabilities.
- The chaos and disruption of an evacuation most likely reward the person making the threat by providing exactly what he or she wanted to begin with.
- The "excitement" and disruption of the typical school day derived from the first threat provide a motivation for copycat incidents.

Evacuation decisions are like closing school for snow—you will never satisfy everyone and the decision will always be second-guessed. Instead of succumbing to pressure from frantic parents, a beleaguered board of education, or a story-hungry media, school administrators need to collaborate with emergency responders to make thoughtful, strategic decisions about responding to bomb threats that are based on a valid assessment of all aspects of the situation. How do you do that? By providing adequate, appropriate training in bomb incident management for all school decision makers.

School administrators need to develop the critical skills necessary to prepare for, prevent, and respond to bomb incidents. All building and district administrators should have the following:

- A functional understanding of explosive devices, sheltering distances, and the disruptive/destructive capabilities of explosive devices.
- An understanding of the protocols and practices that will be employed by emergency responders.
- The ability to appropriately assess the level and validity of threats.
- The ability to identify and analyze pre-attack indicators.
- Protocols in place to prevent future bomb threats and diminish copycat incidents.
- The capability to conduct appropriate and effective searches of school facilities.

States and localities must provide training for bomb incidents that not only is appropriate in terms of the needs of emergency responders but also contains specific strategies, skills, and information for school decision makers. Trainings should focus not just on response after a threat has been determined but also on identifying vulnerabilities and violence- and threat-prevention activities.

At present there are few opportunities nationally for bomb incident–specific training that is appropriate, applicable, or available to educators. Even fewer training opportunities are available that present the necessary content and skills from an educational, not just law enforcement, perspective. At the beginning of this book we mentioned that many of the trainings and resources we reference have been developed by us because they simply don't exist elsewhere. Information about bomb incident training specifically designed for educators is available in the Resources section at www .eschoolsafety.org/resources.

## Final Thoughts

Throughout this book, we have urged educators to view school safety issues proactively. We're ending this chapter by both examining and bemoaning the lack of education-specific resources for preventing and responding to bomb incidents in schools. But that cannot serve as an excuse for not addressing the dramatic increases that are occurring. Here is a list of several things you can do to increase your capabilities in regard to bomb threats and incidents:

- **Find out the facts.** Don't rely on anecdotes, opinions, and overdramatized media reports. Although there isn't a wide array of sources for accurate data and information, some *are* available. Familiarize yourself with the data we have found in our education-specific research, both for the United States as a whole and for your state. Current and past bomb incident reports can be found at www.eschoolsafety.org/bomb-report.

- **Be proactive.** Examine the bomb incident protocols that are currently in your EOP. Are there protocols outlined for bomb threats, suspicious packages, *and* detonations? Review and update these procedures based on the emerging trends noted—in particular, threats from constituents who present themselves in "nontraditional" ways.

- **Collaborate.** Consult and collaborate with local emergency responders to determine best practices. As mentioned before, make sure that this is a two-way conversation. Bomb threats and incidents will almost always require a unified command structure, so all organizations need to be equally involved in planning and protocol development.

- **Don't minimize the threat.** Even though the vast majority of bomb threats never materialize, recognize that threats are more than just an inconvenience or a nuisance—they disrupt instruction, consume valuable financial and personnel resources, create public relations problems, often cause other potential safety problems, and have the potential to traumatize students, staff, and parents.

- **Finally, acknowledge that it's not just about threats.** As with the many other potential threats and vulnerabilities discussed in this book, every school has the potential to be a target for an attack using explosives. We know this because it happens already in U.S. schools. Be sure to develop protocols and implement training for responding to suspicious devices and detonations.

# What to Do After the Initial Response

7

Often school safety resources, publications, and trainings focus on crisis planning and response but ignore the critical activities that must be undertaken at the school level *after* the initial response. In this chapter, we will look at what should be happening in the school after the initial incident response, starting with the need for a comprehensive communications plan to provide information to school stakeholders. We'll also review some considerations and decisions that will need to be made when district-level and communitywide disasters occur. The chapter will close with a brief look at factors that affect the school's response, such as the conflict between staff members' personal and professional responsibilities, dealing with student and parent use of technology during crisis events, and some of the possible implications of litigation and insurance concerns.

To provide a real-world context, let's examine a particularly memorable incident that occurred in Amy's school when she was a principal.

In the late 1990s, my elementary school experienced a situation in which an unknown person entered the building acting erratically and suspiciously. This individual, wearing only one shoe and carrying a large bag, attempted to gain entrance to several of the classrooms. Despite my lack of training at that time, I managed to divert this person's attention and get her to come to my office with me (not a great decision in retrospect, but still better than her being in the classrooms!). I was able to initiate a lockdown of the building (though in a very primitive fashion, using student runners). I ended up with the suspect essentially "trapping" me in my office to listen to her incoherent ramblings and grievances. My secretary called 911 but unfortunately described the incident as a violent, unknown intruder engaged in a hostage situation —which is not how I would have described it. As you can imagine, the law enforcement response (in a small town with little excitement) was swift and dramatic. After the intruder was taken away in cuffs, the crisis event was essentially over. Or was it? More on this in a minute.

## Respond, Then Communicate

Many times in this book we've bemoaned the lack of education-specific crisis response training. We've discussed the need for a comprehensive all-hazards approach to school safety. Of course, we aren't the only ones saying this. Various for-profit and governmental agencies have taken up the mantle of crisis response, most focusing on active shooter situations in schools. There are even a moderate number of resources, both public and private, that provide schools with information about responding to crisis events ranging from natural disasters to medical emergencies. (Some of the ones that we find to be valuable are listed in the Resources section at the end of this book.) Although a focus on crisis response and planning is clearly important, it is equally critical to plan for the activities that need to take place after the initial response, and communication is at the top of the list.

### First, with Staff

When a crisis event occurs in a school, saving lives, mitigating damage, and neutralizing the threat are paramount. Very close behind these activities, however, is the need for effective communication. As the event unfolds and concludes, the needs of a diverse group of stakeholders come to the forefront.

Initially, staff members—first those in the immediate vicinity and then those within the organization—need to know what to do. In previous chapters, we have advocated for a decentralized approach to crisis management that enables individuals to make decisions to respond to a life-or-death event. Clearly, when it is possible to do so, staff members need instructions on what they should be doing, when, and in what fashion. Is the school locked down? Where should the students be? What's going to happen next? This communication needs to come from school leaders or their designees, and it should be clear, specific, and most of all, timely. Although at this point the staff does not need to know every little detail of the event, it is critical that they understand the nature of what occurred, how it will affect them, and what additional activities they need to do to respond. Let's return to Amy's incident:

> In the situation I described, it was not necessary in my initial communication to tell my staff who the person was, what she said, how she acted, or what ended up happening, but it was very important for me to quickly communicate to them that an intruder had come into the school; attempted to reach classrooms; acted in a suspicious, erratic fashion; and been arrested by the police. It was also critical for me to include instructions that classroom doors were to stay locked and students contained in the rooms until the police had finished their investigation.

Let's stop for a moment to quickly discuss a common communication failure—keeping the rest of the organization in the dark. Depending on the size of the district, several organizational entities need to be informed as soon as possible, including district safety personnel, the superintendent, and other relevant directors or supervisors. The nature of the crisis event itself may require a response from the rest of the district, such as locking down other buildings or conducting investigations in other schools. It is also helpful to marshal the resources of the rest of the district to assist with the crisis response and recovery in the affected school.

## Then, with Students

It's important to communicate directly with students as well. We often make the ridiculous assumption that students "don't notice" what's going on. Any parent can tell you that a child who is seemingly not paying attention always manages to overhear the "secret" sidebar conversations in which parents engage, especially if the subject matter is exciting—or better yet, forbidden (or involves ice cream). Students in schools are no different, as even the youngest child is quick to pick up on the heightened tension or flurry of activity caused by even the most minor deviation from routine. For those of you in the northern states, just think how quickly a forecast calling for snow results in rampant speculation about whether school will be cancelled or dismissed early—and that's from the teachers! Even if no particular response procedure is enacted, students will quickly become aware that "something" has happened. Anxiety, speculation, and miscommunication can be minimized by communicating directly with students to provide basic information and assurances. In elementary settings, it is often better to have the teachers communicate directly with their students in a developmentally appropriate fashion, although there is always the potential that the message may not be consistent from teacher to teacher. Again, let's consider Amy's incident:

> In my situation, because some of the students (including my own children) had encountered the intruder early on, it was critical to speak directly to the student body to let them know that the person was no longer in the building and would not be returning, as well as provide a specific assurance of safety. Because my twins were also students, I had the opportunity to reflect on what they needed to hear both as students and as my children. I opted to bring the entire student body together for a brief assembly, allowing me the chance to provide direct reassurance to each student, ensure the consistency of the message, and bring us together both emotionally and physically as a supportive school community.

## Don't Forget the Parents

Some administrators make several critical errors regarding crisis communications and parents. The first is to assume that parents will probably "never know" that this particular event occurred. Wrong. They will always know. You may not know how they will know, and you may not know when, but as they said about the Watergate scandal, *it's not the crime; it's the cover-up.* Informal social networks, social media, and good old-fashioned gossip are powerful forces that can spread either misinformation or reassurance in record time. It is foolish to allow rumors and false reports to proliferate rather than provide good, accurate information about an event that occurred and how the school responded to protect children. Ultimately, parents have a right to know what occurred in their children's school, as well as what has been done about it. Need a litmus test? Would you want to know if this particular event occurred in your child's school? If you answered yes, then the parents in your school need to be adequately informed. Here's Amy's experience with the parent communication portion of her incident:

> The duality of my role as both principal and parent made my communication with parents about this incident a given. The letter that was sent home with students that afternoon briefly summarized not only what had transpired, but more important, how we responded and what we were doing to protect our students. I closed with an invitation to call or meet with me for additional information or to address any concerns. Our midmorning assembly seemed to bring closure to the incident as far as our students were concerned; a carefully crafted explanation appeared to do the same for parents.

**While You Were Responding . . .**

Now that we've convinced you that you must clearly communicate directly with parents, let's talk about the second potential error—assuming that you have plenty of time to investigate what happened, craft a message that presents it in the best possible light, and effectively communicate it to parents. Wrong again. While you're drafting your initial communication to your staff (as described earlier), one of your students is texting his parents with a garbled version of what occurred. As you send out that staff e-mail or make that general announcement, that parent is calling other parents to find out "what happened." When you're talking with your students, the community member who was listening to the police radio is calling the board office or (even worse) the local television station to either notify them or try to get more information. Let's revisit Amy's experience:

> Because the incident was dispatched as a "hostage" situation, word spread quickly among local volunteer responders, as well as to the media, who quickly picked up on the potential drama because of the number of units being dispatched. A well-placed phone call from a parent who was in the building at the time dropping off her children boosted the level of panic among the neighborhood parents who were

"in the know." By the time I had finished talking with the investigating officer and thought about what to say to my staff, multiple parents had already showed up in the office, one television station had called, and another had set up a camera at the edge of the playground. Could I really have entertained any notion that parents would be unaware of the incident until I told them at my leisure?

Keep in mind that this incident occurred before mass-notification systems, social media, and other innovations that have compressed the window of opportunity for communication even further. In my situation, even though there were some panicked parents and frantic phone calls, the vast majority of parents were informed at the end of the day when my letter arrived home with their child. This is not always an option today.

So, how can an administrator respond to a crisis event *and* communicate effectively about it within a brief amount of time? Here are some suggestions:

1. **Focus on responding before anything else.** Despite what we've said in this chapter, your primary responsibility is ensuring the safety and well-being of your students and staff. Don't compromise an effective, appropriate response by being distracted by the need to tell everyone about it. People clearly want information, and they want it now. But sometimes they just have to wait until everyone is safe.

2. **Make a plan for communication part of your EOP** so that you're ready before the crisis event occurs. Clearly establish and communicate to stakeholders the way in which crisis communications will occur and how they can best access the information they need. Automated calls or text messages, e-mails, website updates, or even letters sent home with students may all be options, but let parents and staff know in advance how you will be communicating with them.

3. **Take time now to craft effective templates for communication** that can be quickly edited and disseminated. In the heat of the moment, you will most likely not remember all of the components that need to be addressed with staff, students, and parents. We recommend that school leaders collaborate districtwide to craft fill-in-the-blank

templates for both written and verbal notifications that are comprehensive and consistent for all schools. Sample emergency communication templates are available in the Resource section at www.echoolsafety.org/resources.

Now might be a good time to stop and talk about communication issues from a more pragmatic standpoint. Nearly every school district has (or should have) policies about communicating during crisis events. In many cases, communication to staff and parents often originates at the building level, from the building administrator or a designee. Leadership teams should determine in advance how (and to what extent) building-level administrators will brief and update the stakeholders in their school. Communication with the media, press releases, and briefings are almost always handled by the superintendent or a district-level designee in conjunction with the public information officer (PIO) of the emergency response agencies involved. If your district has a PIO, work with that individual beforehand to determine who will craft and deliver press releases, statements, and other communication to the media.

Although the circumstances of the crisis incident will dictate the exact nature of communication with stakeholders, here are some things to consider:

- **Provide a brief description of the incident and its impact.** Be as specific as possible (overly vague descriptions allow room for mental embellishments and rumor-mongering), but avoid individual details, such as names or other specific identifying information. Stay away from overly dramatic phrases ("a crazed intruder" versus an "unauthorized individual") and opinions about what happened ("students panicked"), keeping the primary focus on the facts. On the other hand, if the situation was serious, scary, or chaotic, don't minimize it, as you'll lose credibility.
- **Don't provide an assurance of safety until you actually have one**. Communicating that "everything is fine" or "all students are safe" when you haven't really accounted for all students is irresponsible.
- **Discuss the school's response to the incident, focusing on what was done to protect the students and ensure their safety,** and provide an update as to the current status of the school and students.

- **Provide direction, specifying what you need students, parents, staff, and community members to do—and not do.** This is easier and more effective if you have provided information and training about crisis response before the chaos and anxiety of an actual event.

Above all, discuss and coordinate communication plans, templates, procedures, and methodology far in advance. When it comes to communication, the key words are *frequent, ongoing, accurate,* and *consistent.* Nothing takes a situation from bad to worse more than rumors, misinformation, or radio silence.

## Considerations for District-Level and Communitywide Disasters

Up until now, most of our discussion has assumed that the crisis event has occurred within and is affecting just the individual school. Although this may be the case in many of the incidents you will face, there is a strong possibility that the crisis event you are dealing with is a district- or community-level event. The wildfire that is threatening your school is most likely also affecting the rest of the community, at least in that vicinity. That tornado isn't just going to swoop down over one school; it is a threat to all of the immediate area. So what are the implications of a districtwide or communitywide disaster versus a more localized problem?

### Roles and Responsibilities When Emergency Responders Aren't Available

Almost every crisis response procedure delineates the roles and responsibilities of responders. Short-sighted plans outline these procedures until the point at which emergency responders (law enforcement, firefighters, emergency medical services) arrive. But what if they aren't able to arrive? Although the amount of time before emergency responders arrive may vary depending on your geographic location and other factors, in our minds, we are always counting on being able to quickly turn over the reins of crisis response to the "professionals." In a disaster or communitywide crisis event, however, the scope and severity as well as the nature of the event may prevent emergency responders from coming to your aid for quite some time. Whether it's a physical issue (the roads to the school are flooded or blocked with debris) or a resource problem (the existing resources of emergency responders are overwhelmed by the riot or the fire), it is possible that the school will need to initiate and sustain an emergency response without the aid of traditional first responders.

A few years ago, a school just a few miles from our house was completely destroyed in a tornado on the eve of graduation. Luckily, the tornado struck in the evening, and there were just a few people on site, but the devastation was tremendous. But it wasn't just the school. The police station down the road was destroyed, along with all the department's police cars that weren't out on patrol. The fire department lost several vehicles that were in the path of the tornado. Numerous houses in the community were destroyed and multiple people died, including a driver in a car in front of the school. Now imagine that this catastrophic event had happened during the day, with a building full of children. Police and fire personnel would not be coming, at least not soon, because they would be physically unable to reach the school and would need to bring in resources from surrounding areas.

The takeaway here is that your crisis response plan has to be collaborative and include emergency responders, but it cannot be completely based on their immediate presence. We need to plan for what to do in the immediate minutes following an event, but we also need a plan that extends beyond that to include things like food, shelter, and communication in a community-based disaster.

## Family Emergency Plans for Staff

Another element of this larger-scope planning that is often neglected is family emergency plans. A few years ago, we had the experience of being in Atlanta during a snow event. (We're not calling it a snowstorm because by our Ohioan standards it wasn't!) In the resulting traffic and other weather-related chaos that ensued, some schools ended up with students stranded overnight. Although this may be every teacher's nightmare, in this case, it revealed a brutal reality for administrators, as there were many, many, students, but not many staff members. Why? Because many of the staff had left. Now, we're not knocking educators for choosing to take care of the needs of their own families, but we are suggesting that they have an equally important moral and professional responsibility to the students in their immediate care. Think of the dilemma here—there's a crisis event occurring that affects your school and makes it necessary for you to see to student and staff needs, yet your own children or family are also affected by this event. It's an impossible conversation to have in the middle of a high-stress event, yet it is critical to have adequate staff to ensure the safety and security of the students. The dangerous end result of failing to plan for such an event is a school full of students under the care of just the few adults who haven't left the building.

Our recommendation is to discuss this issue *before* a crisis event occurs. It's important for educators to consider that their professional responsibilities extend beyond the school day and can supersede personal factors. Like emergency responders, all school staff members should be encouraged or and even required to develop family emergency plans at the start of each school year. Planning assistance is available at www.ready.gov and will ensure that staff members' families are provided for in a crisis event, allowing them to focus on and fulfill their responsibilities at the school. Additional information, as well as a template for a family emergency plan, is available in the Resources section at www.eschoolsafety.org/resources.

## Use—and Misuse—of Technology and Social Media During Crisis Response

If your school experiences a crisis event, students (and adults!) will be talking about it on social media. The reality is that in addition to the other duties enumerated in this chapter, educators and administrators must be prepared to deal with the consequences of what is being discussed and shared online.

Before you think "No phones!" remember that it is completely unrealistic (and, frankly, foolhardy) to expect students not to use their technology devices during, and especially after, a crisis event. Students who have physical access to such devices are likely to use them. Instead of wasting time, energy, and effort trying to curb this inevitable use, a more effective approach is to talk to students about the possible unintended consequences of sharing and help them distinguish between technology use that helps and technology use that harms.

From 2012 to 2014, we researched and documented students' use of social media during and after school shootings in the United States. Our findings were striking. Many students were, in essence, live-tweeting the violent events that were happening in their schools as they were unfolding (e.g., "We're on lockdown" "Three people were shot at and two were shot. I'm freaking out" "I'm freaking out, like, I don't know what to do" "Somebody was shot at our school!"). During the shooting event in Chardon, Ohio, in 2012, a student was imploring others to "pray for Chardon" while the shooter was still *inside* the school. The instances in which students tweet or post that they are actively in lockdown for a violent event are almost innumerable. An obvious question is, what safety responses are these students *not* doing because they are so busy on their phones?

Another typical behavior is for students to pass along information during and after the event. Although this activity may seem innocuous, adults are left to deal with the potentially far-reaching consequences of information—accurate and inaccurate—that is leaked. In our research, we saw students "reporting" who and how many people had been shot and posting photos of the victims as well as the alleged perpetrators. The danger comes when students' posts and tweets become news—sometimes at the national level.

When a student posted a screenshot on Instagram of a private text-message conversation about another student who died, it was widely circulated as part of the media coverage of the shooting. In one particular instance, a student tweeted the name of a classmate who had been shot and killed. We can't ascribe malicious intent to this teenager, who certainly was just passing along sad information to classmates. However, because this teen's Twitter account was public (which is the default mode), the news media were able to see the tweet and report on the news of the death. As a result, the parents of the student who was killed found out about their child's death on the news, because the administration hadn't had time to locate the parents to tell them in person.

We know that forbidding the use of technology isn't possible, so what can be done? Teachers, administrators, and parents must have conversations with students about the responsible use of technology during and after crisis events. When a crisis event occurs, students should be encouraged to check in with their parents and guardians—with a few caveats: namely, that communicating with parents is only appropriate *after* it is safe to do so, not in the middle of an ongoing crisis. Be specific with your instructions: a check-in isn't a 25-minute phone call or a 200-message exchange detailing the grievances of how the school handled the event or the injustice of having to leave a lunchbox behind during evacuation for a credible bomb threat.

Explain to students the potential dangers of broadcasting sensitive information. In the aftermath of a crisis event, everything, including student use of social media, will be examined under a microscope by law enforcement, insurance companies, and the media. These crisis-specific concerns can easily be folded into discussions you should already be having with students about digital citizenship and responsible use of social media.

Although we have focused here on technology use by students, be aware that parents and even school staff are just as capable of acting foolishly on the internet. The issues and concerns we've just outlined for students can, and should be, applied equally to parents, staff, and community members. Administrators and educators must be prepared to deal with the ramifications of countless discussions on social media.

## Litigation and Insurance

When a crisis event occurs in a school, the school should expect to be sued. It is important to remember the distinction between being sued and losing a costly lawsuit. The former is nearly inevitable; the latter is not. Avoiding litigation should never be the motivation for any actions or responses, nor is it part of any advice in this book. Although the work of making schools safer is being undertaken for moral and ethical reasons, it has the side effect of reducing the potential liability of the school.

In the aftermath of a school crisis event, documentation is critical yet often overlooked. In the diagram of the incident command structure shown in Figure 3.3 on page 47, the Finance/Administration section is tasked with keeping financial records, but its primary duty is a broader form of record keeping and documentation. A detailed, minute-by-minute account of what happened may seem unimportant compared to the other needs you are facing, but the school district's insurer will need this information, and it will be critical evidence during any litigation that follows. It's crucial to designate (in advance, and with redundancy) someone who will note important details (as soon as it is safe to do so) pertaining to locations, injuries, damage, and so on, as well as the disposition of these items (e.g., what hospitals victims were sent to, what responders were on-site, what areas needed to be secured).

## Help Is on the Way—and Sometimes *in* the Way

Whether the crisis event is school-based or community-wide, past incidents have clearly demonstrated that the immediate aftermath will bring an outpouring of offers for assistance and support. When we talk with school leaders and emergency responders about this tidal wave of assistance, it seems to be sometimes both a blessing and a curse.

In the Ohio tornado incident described earlier, within a few hours of the destruction, school leaders had offers from the local community college to use its facilities for graduation and summer classes, were loaned modular classrooms and trailers for administrative offices, had a fencing company secure the school site, and were provided with a seemingly unending supply of food for staff and first responders. They also had a barrage of sales calls from opportunistic contractors, trainers, media consultants, and others, along with literally dozens of curious reporters and gawkers trying to gain access to the wreckage.

The more media attention or notoriety an event engenders, the more both sides of the coin are shown. The tragedy at Sandy Hook resulted in a tremendous outpouring of financial and tangible assistance that had a positive effect on a devastated community. It also engendered more horrifying acts like conspiracy-inspired videos and "safety experts" photographing themselves in front of the killer's house for promotional materials. After a 2017 shooting at a high school in the state of Washington, two individuals were charged with stealing purses from the cars abandoned by panicked parents in the school parking lot. In that same event, one set of parents were "pranked" with fake text-message notifications that their daughter had been killed in the school. Fortunately, almost without exception, organizations that have experienced tragedies, big and small, report an incredible level of support and compassion directed their way.

In any crisis event, many well-meaning individuals will arrive, most of whom can provide valuable assistance. As illustrated by the examples just mentioned, a few people may also show up who have opportunistic (at best) and criminal (at worst) intent. The school must be prepared to deal with both. Make sure your crisis plan (and subsequent training) deals with what volunteers can and cannot do, who will coordinate and supervise their efforts, and when these procedures will begin and end. Again, Amy's recollection is relevant:

The story of my confused intruder has a happy ending in that, beyond a few frayed nerves, everything turned out OK. At the time, I did the best I could with the abilities and information that I had, but it often occurs to me now how the situation could have turned out so differently if just one of the variables had changed. What if the intruder had turned violent? What if there had been a weapon in that duffel bag? My lack of training and the ability to think like a first responder left the outcome of this incident more to chance than to anything else, and that should never be the case when the safety of our children may be on the line.

We often hear from educators in our trainings that they are afraid they will do the wrong thing in their response to a crisis event. Although this is a legitimate concern that illustrates the need for appropriate, ongoing training, our response is pretty much always the same: no response will ever be perfect. The event will not proceed as imagined. People will forget to do something they should (or shouldn't) do. Communication will be spotty. Emotions will run high and chaos may reign. But that doesn't negate the need for us to do our best to respond—in fact, it only makes the need more critical. The goal is not perfection but protection. There are really only two egregious mistakes you can make: deluding yourself into believing that "it won't happen here" and doing nothing when it does.

## Moving from Theory to Practice

Now that we've had a general discussion about responding, let's apply those concepts specifically to a given timeline for incident response. Earlier in this chapter, we looked at each issue in isolation; now let's examine these same issues collectively across the spectrum of time after an incident begins to examine what should be occurring or considered in the first minutes, hours, and days after a crisis event.

### It's Not Over Until It's Over

The roles and responsibilities of effective crisis management extend far beyond the short duration of the actual event, primarily because the potential for harm continues beyond the immediate threat.

Take a car accident, for example. Two cars collide on a busy highway. The occupants have survived with a few cuts and bruises, but the threat is not over. Although serious injuries and death didn't occur in the event itself (the crash), they are still possible. The cars are sitting motionless in the lanes of a highway while unaware motorists approach them at rapid speed, creating the potential for an additional accident. The drivers have gotten out of their cars but are standing next to their vehicles, making them even more vulnerable. The "minor" aches and pains one driver is experiencing may be a sign of serious internal bleeding. Even when emergency responders arrive, there are still additional safety concerns that must be addressed. The emergency vehicles are parked in a way to protect the responders, while police officers divert traffic away from the scene. The cars are leaking gasoline, so a perimeter is established and everyone is moved safely away.

Now apply that series of considerations to a school. Because of a lack of training and experience with crisis events, educators have a tendency to see the immediate problem as only the event itself. Although the initial problem may have been resolved (the unknown intruder has run out of the building, the storm has passed, the angry parent has agreed to meet with the principal), additional threats remain. Was that the only intruder? Are there others in the building? Has the storm weakened any of the school structures? Are there threats from debris or broken glass? Has the angry parent gone to his car for a gun? How can the safety of the person meeting with him be ensured? After the initial event, the school must still respond to ensure the safety of the staff, students, and facility. You cannot breathe a sigh of relief and "get back to work" until you have looked at the entire response timeline.

## In the First Minutes

As the event unfolds, communication is sketchy, often inaccurate, and most likely not even occurring. As a responder, you must assess what *is* known and initiate the proper response protocol. What you cannot do is remain passive as the room fills with smoke, hoping that someone will give instructions. You must immediately overcome the normalcy bias that was discussed in Chapter 1. Yes—this really could be happening! Here is where the critical importance of training is most apparent. (For more information on training, consult the Resources section at www.eschoolsafety.org.) Now is not the time to dig through desk drawers looking for an unwieldy, out-dated crisis notebook and flip frantically through the pages for guidance. This is the time to *know* what to do. You need to quickly make, and most likely initiate, a plan for the current threat based on what has been said (if anything) and what can be immediately observed. You must act quickly and decisively, as the biggest mistake is not doing anything!

In general, you want to move to a place of safety, whether that is making the current space safer (moving away from windows, locking the door) or moving away from the threat by evacuating. The more potentially deadly the threat, the quicker the response must be. You may have a 10-minute warning of the approaching tornado or 30 seconds of hearing gunshots before a shooter attempts to enter the room, but you must do something. Accounting for the students in your immediate care should be a priority. This is not the time to go looking for a single missing student, putting the majority at risk, but you want to do the best you can to cast a wide net that accounts for as many students and staff as possible.

## In the First Hour

Depending on the event, the initial threat may have been resolved relatively quickly. Now is the time to consider secondary threats. Has the original problem created consequences that need to be addressed? Are there new threats to deal with? These might include an unsecured perimeter, damage to the facilities, the need to relocate, or the need to provide first aid. The health, safety, and security of everyone in the building must be accounted for during this time. Identify who is missing, who is injured, and who needs assistance of some kind. Communication becomes increasingly frequent and more important during this time. Staff members need to be provided with information and instructions and must also communicate their status and needs to decision makers. Parents, media, and other school stakeholders will start to make demands for information either by phone or by their possible physical presence on-site.

## In Subsequent Hours

The nature of the crisis event will most likely dictate the actions that must be taken after the initial response. At a minimum, information must be provided to school stakeholders, along with assurances of safety and instructions on what to do next. A detailed account of the status of all the people involved or affected by the crisis event must be established and acted upon. Liaisons or contact people need to be deployed around the rapidly expanding "ring" of those aware of or involved in the incident. Someone needs to be at the hospital with injured students, someone needs to be providing information and instructions to staff and parents, someone needs to be interacting with the media, and so on. These roles and responsibilities need to be determined (and trained for) far in advance of the incident as part of the EOP.

There are logistical concerns during this time as well. Is the facility still safe? Where will students be moved? What should students be doing? How will the physical and emotional safety needs that will occur be addressed? How will necessary daily functions such as restrooms, supervision, lunches, transportation, collecting belongings, and other concerns be handled? Most likely, parent reunification will be taking place during this time, creating a whole new set of concerns and constraints that we'll discuss in the next chapter.

## Everything Else That's Happening While You're Responding

So far we've addressed the concerns that are within the control (to some degree) of school personnel and emergency responders. The ugly truth is that while you are busy responding, the rest of the world doesn't stop. In fact, depending on the nature, severity, and effectiveness of the response, outside factors can intensify exponentially. While you're separating the combatants in the cafeteria brawl, treating the injured, and interviewing witnesses, students are uploading videos of the fight to social media, texting their parents (quite possibly with inaccurate information), tweeting at the local television station in hopes of getting interviewed, and vowing retaliation online. Parents are calling each other, heading to the building, and criticizing the lack of information coming from the school. Meanwhile on social media, anonymous actors are stirring the pot with inflammatory comments and false information. And many others, whether they are involved or not, are "helping" by spreading conjectures about who did what to whom.

Unfortunately, there isn't a great deal that you can do to stop these forces, but there are some strategies for mitigating the concerns. Not surprisingly, the most important tools are those we've referenced over and over in this book—training and communication. When staff, students, and parents have been trained and understand their roles and responsibilities, they will be fulfilling those functions rather than engaging in idle speculation. Much of the rumor and misinformation arises from a lack of communication from those who *do* know what is going on. Accurate, frequent, specific communication to all stakeholders needs to be a continual priority. We rarely see educational leaders being criticized and condemned by the parents and community for communicating too much, but we frequently see administrators accused of withholding information or not informing parents.

Simply being aware of and sensitive to these outside factors and what you're up against is important, but keep in mind, your most critical responsibility is what is happening in front of you in your building. You cannot prevent the Monday-morning quarterbacking, but you can ensure that you have done the best you possibly could in a bad situation.

Without adequate consideration and planning beyond just the initial crisis event itself, the struggle to provide for physical safety, emotional security, and adequate communication and to initiate the recovery process will be much more difficult. In many cases, the ripple effect of associated problems may be worse than the actual event itself.

Let's examine how such a situation might unfold. The school has a minor boiler malfunction that results in the need to evacuate the school. No communication is sent out, but the rumor mill circulates a story that there was an explosion at the building. Panicked parents rush to the school, where there is no plan or procedure to deal with the traffic or the chaos. Because there is no formalized evacuation plan, a student crossing the parking lot to the evacuation site is struck by a car racing to the school, and a parent is injured in the traffic accident.

The lesson here is simple: You must carefully plan for and consider your actions in the minutes and hours after the incident to avoid a crisis *after* the crisis.

# Recovering, Reflecting, and Learning

8

This last chapter examines some of the final aspects of emergency response. We'll start the discussion with an examination of short-term recovery activities such as reunifying parents with students, resuming operations, reestablishing physical and emotional safety, providing appropriate mental health supports and interventions, and identifying at-risk individuals in the wake of the incident. Then we'll move on to longer-term recovery and response issues. We'll conclude with some suggestions for debriefing, reflecting, and updating policies and procedures for incorporation into future planning and training.

## Short-Term Recovery

Crisis intervention and recovery takes place in two general stages: short-term recovery and long-term recovery. Because the first priority of recovery is to ensure physical safety, short-term recovery really begins when a response protocol is enacted. Rapidly evacuating from the building after the boiler explodes is both a critical response procedure and a short-term recovery activity as it removes students from the threat and ensures their physical safety. Other short-term recovery activities begin in the minutes and hours after a crisis event. School and emergency response decision makers need to determine the scope, severity, and impact of the crisis event. What happened? Who was affected? How severely? What needs are present? What is the current status of the school and its occupants?

Although we've already discussed the need to provide for basic human needs (food, water, shelter), short-term recovery planning should also address the following:

- Strategies to mitigate the trauma of the event by minimizing student exposure to frightening or traumatic images, through means such as separating medical triage areas from student evacuation routes or moving students to unaffected areas of the school. Although many educators (including ourselves) aren't experts on providing mental health supports and interventions, the good news is that there are professional resources, agencies, and individuals that are. It is not necessary or appropriate for school leaders to be mental health professionals, but it is necessary and appropriate for them to prepare and plan to access these services for those who are affected.
- Establishing communication protocols that disseminate enough information to provide assurances, yet limit students' exposure to the media and media reports (Brock et al., 2009).
- Providing for the physical health and safety of students with special needs, disabilities, or chronic illnesses, including provisions for assistance devices, medications, and appropriate caregivers. Be sure to collaborate with special education directors, school nurses, and others to proactively plan for the unique needs of these constituents both during and after a crisis event.

## Critical Activities in Short-Term Recovery

As we discuss these critical recovery activities, examine a copy of your school or district's EOP and evaluate whether the following elements have been adequately addressed:

- **Reestablishing security—*Secure the site or perimeter, cordoning off areas with immediate hazards and implementing sufficient supervision and protection.*** In the aftermath of an event, additional protections must be immediately put into place as the facility itself, as well as its occupants, is at greater risk. It cannot always be assumed that the resolution of a specific incident means that all other threats or hazards have been addressed or eliminated.

- **Meeting basic physical needs—*Provide first aid, shelter, food, and water.*** Students or staff may need to be treated for minor injuries, moved out of harm's way, or sheltered from the elements. Treating shock with blankets, providing food and water, and moving students into a common area for supervision and support all need to occur immediately after the event.

- **Meeting immediate emotional needs—*Provide assurance of safety, physical contact, and personal interaction.*** Because of the vulnerable populations within a school, this aspect is critical. Students need to see a familiar face and be given a reassuring word or touch. It is important to quickly identify and respond to acute emotional needs of certain individuals—for example, the sibling of a victim, the student who witnessed the assault, the teacher whose student was injured.

- **Accounting for staff and students—*Determine the location and status of all stakeholders.*** Although we have dealt with accountability as an integral component of specific emergency responses, in many cases the crisis incident and its response occur so quickly that there has not been time to accurately account for staff and students. As soon as the crisis ends, the school must quickly and accurately account for everyone who was in the building when the event started. This means that accountability systems for staff and students need to be in place and readily available. Keep in mind that depending on the nature of the event, power and internet access may not be available. Having both high- and low-tech systems in place is critical. Don't forget other people who may have been in the building during the event, such as parents, visitors, and personnel from other agencies. That's one more reason why consistent, accurate visitor sign-in procedures are important.

## Operational Considerations

As recovery begins, critical decisions will need to be made about the facility and its inhabitants. These include the following:

1. The status of the physical plant:
   - Is the building habitable?

- What decision makers in the incident command structure currently have authority over the building? Police? Fire? The principal?
- What are the physical, personnel, and equipment needs (such as repairs, security, generators, etc.)?
- When will it be possible to resume operations? Depending on the nature of the event, it may not be possible to reoccupy the building or resume operations at the physical site for an extended period of time. This is when a continuity of operations plan (COOP) is activated as part of the long-term recovery activities. A COOP provides a detailed description of the decisions and activities required to quickly and effectively resume essential operations. Additional information on developing a COOP can be found in the Resources section at www.eschoolsafety .org/resources.

2. The status of school stakeholders:
    - Should the school day continue? What modifications or procedures need to be put in place to do so?
    - Should students be dismissed? If so, will the parent reunification plan be activated? (See below for more on this.)
    - What physical and emotional supports need to be put in place for staff members? Depending on the event and its impact, a staff meeting may be valuable, allowing for direct communication and debriefing as well as planning the initiation and implementation of recovery activities.

## Communicating with Stakeholders

Providing updates and information to other responders, staff, parents, and the media is one of most critical but often overlooked short-term recovery activities. Although we have discussed communication in previous chapters, the importance of timely, accurate communication in the immediate aftermath of the event cannot be overstated. The staff members need to know what they should do next. Where should they go? What should they do with their students? What are their responsibilities? In addition, they need to have at least a cursory knowledge of what happened, as well as the scope of the impact. If decision makers do not provide adequate information, stakeholders will seek to acquire the information they need elsewhere—through outside sources that could be inaccurate, misleading, or purely speculative.

Students need to have some information about what has occurred and, more important, about what is being done to keep them safe. Communication to parents needs to be swift and ongoing. Uncertain, uninformed parents create mayhem and confusion in what is already a chaotic situation. Keep in mind that translation services may be needed for some parents. More important, after ensuring the safety of students, it should be every educator's top priority to provide parents with information about their student's well-being.

Finally, communication with the media should be seen not as an adversarial undertaking, but rather as another means to get necessary information out to stakeholders and community members. Designating a public information officer (PIO) or spokesperson in advance is always a good idea, but keep in mind that the nature of the event may dictate who is available to speak or which responding agency needs to take the lead in communicating with the media.

## Reunification with Parents or Guardians

Parent reunification is the means by which students are reunified with their parents or guardians after a traumatic event. Sounds simple, doesn't it? After all, parent-student reunification takes place every day when school dismisses. But obviously things are different in the aftermath of a crisis. Begin with the emotional anxiety of parents who know something bad has happened at the school but do not know if their child is all right. Now add the physical and emotional chaos and confusion created by a crisis event as it takes its toll on traumatized students, overwhelmed staff, and frantic parents. Finally, add in dozens of reporters scrambling for information, interviews, and photos. Failure to plan for this situation is a recipe for a disaster after the disaster.

In some instances, parent reunification occurs when a traumatic event disrupts the school day to such an extent that students are better served by being sent home to the support of their parents. Parent reunification may be required if the school is unsafe to occupy, such as after a fire, during a bomb threat, or as a result of an act of violence. Although parent reunification can take place within the school itself, quite often students are moved to an off-site location to be reunited with their parents.

Parent reunification presents a number of logistical challenges that must be dealt with in advance. Where will an entire school full of students shelter if the school is uninhabitable? How will the students be moved to that facility? What areas in the facility will be used and for what purposes? Are there areas for check-in, screening, counseling, and reunification? Is there adequate parking for literally hundreds of cars? How will a crowd of anxious parents be directed, screened, and managed? How will the school ensure (and document) that a child is released only to approved, custodial parents? Who will provide adequate supervision and support for a multitude of anxious, traumatized students?

We work with schools that take safety very seriously. When we have completed our work, they have developed, reviewed, and revised a comprehensive EOP, trained their staff and students on how to effectively respond to crisis events, and put this theory into practice through drills. When they skip over the parent reunification plan, however, even these "poster child" schools fail to adequately understand the ramifications of not having an effective means to deal with the aftermath of a crisis event. Despite their best efforts, their children and their organization are still at risk.

We know from parents that lacking a plan to reunify parents with students can add to already unimaginable trauma. This was graphically illustrated in the heartbreaking scene after the murder of 26 people at Sandy Hook Elementary. As one parent who lost a child that day described the situation, "One of the most stressful things that day was reunification. We were told by three different people to look for our daughter at three different places. The chaos made it so much worse for all of us" (Save the Children, 2013, p. 6).

The good news is that planning for parent reunification is fairly straightforward, as it is essentially a logistical exercise. Numerous resources exist to help with reunification planning, such as FEMA's "dual gate" parent reunification method and the standard reunification method from the "I Love U Guys" Foundation (Keyes, 2011), which is based on practices used by the Adams 12 Five-Star School District in Colorado. (A standard reunification method is available in the Resources section at www.eschoolsafety.org.)

The most critical thing to remember is that planning for reunifying parents with students *must* be done in advance. Not planning in advance creates significant liabilities, as it ignores mental health concerns, responsibilities for accounting for students, and maintaining or reestablishing the chain of custody. The costs of creating and implementing an effective parent reunification plan, in terms of materials and planning, are minimal, especially when compared to the catastrophic costs of not preparing for reunification. The Educator's School Safety Network provides training for creating and implementing a parent reunification plan. See the Resources section at www.eschoolsafety.org/resources for more information.

## Long-Term Recovery

Long-term recovery occurs in the days, weeks, and months after an event. Addressing the long-term impact of crisis events is an effective approach to mitigating the inevitable consequences. Long-term, ongoing recovery activities help the school return to normalcy more rapidly and provide opportunities to ensure the continued safety of the organization. Just as in short-term recovery, long-term recovery activities should address communication, debriefing and evaluation, and operational, psychological, and social-support concerns.

### Communicating with Stakeholders

A communications plan is critical to long-term recovery. Staff members should have frequent updates about the myriad of issues associated with the crisis event, such as when school will resume, what they can do to assist, what supports will be available, the status of those injured, and so on. Parent and community members need to have accurate, timely information related to the ways in which the crisis event has affected them and their families. There is often an outpouring of support and the desire to "do something," which can be more effectively channeled with proper communication.

After the initial reporting of the crisis events, local (and sometimes national) media will be in search of "new" information or other angles of the story. Without appropriate communication from the school, the media will find alternate, less reliable, and sometimes more damaging sources for news to report.

## Debriefing and Evaluation

Despite the fatigue, emotion, and stress of the response to the crisis event, it is important to debrief and evaluate discrete components of the school's or district's response as well as the overall effectiveness of the crisis-related activities. How did the communication plan work? Were all students and staff accurately accounted for? Were the response protocols effective? What worked as planned? What didn't? There is always much to be learned from both a limited "hot" debrief immediately following the response, and a more comprehensive review as part of the school's long-term recovery. It's important that these debriefing activities provide critical, objective insights into what worked and what didn't, without devolving into criticism and assigning blame. The point of debriefing is to improve the planning, prevention, and response to the next crisis event.

## Resuming Operations

In short-term recovery, operational decisions typically center on the status of the building and whether classes can continue. Long-term recovery requires decisions to be made about when to return to school; what maintenance, planning, and support activities must be completed to be able to resume operations; and how to transition students back into the post-crisis environment. Other less obvious concerns will also affect the resumption of daily operations, such as funerals, hospital visitations, memorial events, community support activities, and replacing staff, materials, or equipment.

## Mental Health Counseling and Support

Not all people exposed to a crisis event will be affected in the same way, so different individuals require interventions that vary in scope and intensity. Some individuals may need no support at all, whereas others (in particular, those with pre-existing conditions or dispositions) will need more intensive services (NIMH, 2001). The need for support services is not always directly related to individuals' exposure or proximity to the crisis event. Factors such as physical and emotional proximity to the crisis, as well as personal vulnerability factors, can be predictors of psychological trauma, but some people may need additional support even without those traditional markers (Brock et al., 2009). As a result, crisis intervention practices need to be tailored to address individual, specific needs and, more significantly, should allow for individuals to manage their response to the crisis event without assistance (Brock et al., 2009). It's important (and heartening) to note that according to the National Institute of Mental Health, recovery from a crisis event is the norm, not the exception (NIMH, 2001).

### Establishing and Providing Social Supports

It is important to identify all those affected by the crisis event and provide appropriate supports and interventions. One excellent resource for recovery planning is the National Association of School Psychologists' PREPaRE model (see the Resources section at www.eschoolsaftey.org for additional information). The PREPaRE model provides a list of activities and initiatives that schools can implement as part of long-term recovery to foster social support for stakeholders. These include the following:

- Returning students to familiar school routines and environments.
- Reuniting students with established caregivers, classmates, and teachers.
- Training and empowering caregivers and educators to provide crisis recovery support (Brock et al., 2009).

You'll notice that mental health supports are often mentioned but little discussed in this chapter. This is intentional. We are educators and safety experts, not mental health professionals. We would never presume to diagnose, prescribe, or treat the critical social and emotional needs that are present in individuals who have experienced a traumatic event, and neither should you. But that doesn't mean we can ignore them either. The role of educators in this regard is to locate and facilitate appropriate mental health support. Although we do not train in or provide mental health services related to recovery, we have gathered some of the best information available into a repository for your use in the Resources section at www.eschoolsafety.org/resources.

## Things to Think About

A significant part of this chapter has focused on facilitating the recovery of students after a traumatic event—as it should. We would be remiss, however, not to mention the absolute necessity of planning for and preparing to deal with the impact of a crisis event on the school staff. Teachers, administrators, and support staff often suffer a dual impact from a crisis event. They were most likely involved in the immediate response to the event, had a high level of exposure to the trauma, and must subordinate their physical and emotional pain in order to protect and support the students in their care. Educational leaders need to provide equal attention to specific plans and arrangements for staff debriefing, communication, respite, and support systems.

Finally, remember that a crisis event does not need to occur within the four walls of the school for its impact to be felt. The death of a student in a car accident, a community devastated by a flash flood, a family killed in a fire—all will affect the school regardless of where the incident occurred. The recovery planning team must initiate recovery and support activities that address the various levels of trauma in the school. In short, without the necessary recovery measures, the scope and impact of the crisis event increase.

## Moving Forward: Lessons Learned

So the crisis event has occurred. You've responded. Help has arrived and the event is over. The injured have been cared for; the perpetrators have been caught. Witnesses have been interviewed and students reunited with their parents. The school can now get back to "normal." Or can it?

After a crisis event (big or small), it is not possible to just go back to business as usual. Every incident response presents a variety of opportunities that must be seized, including the following:

- **The opportunity to debrief.** All those involved or affected by the event need to be heard and to reflect on what took place. What went well? What didn't? What was unexpected? What worked? What deficiencies were clearly present? Debriefing should take place as soon as possible and shouldn't just involve key decision makers or those closest to the event. Safety teams, administrative teams, staff, students, and parents should all have an opportunity to process and reflect on how crisis prevention and response can be improved.
- **The opportunity to make changes.** Debriefing is not venting. It's not just an opportunity to rant or criticize; it's a chance to make things better. The results of debriefing activities become the foundation for improvement. But you can't just admire the problem; you need to make specific, concrete changes in training, resources, facilities,

personnel, and the EOP itself that reflect the deficiencies that were obvious in the heat of the moment.

- **The opportunity to preserve what worked.** Debriefing also demonstrates what needs to stay the same. What isn't broken and doesn't need to be fixed? What policies, procedures, plans, and people worked exactly as they were supposed to? How does one ensure that what worked will be effective next time?

## Some Closing Thoughts

The work of school safety is vital. It must be approached in a comprehensive, strategic, ongoing fashion. Most important, keeping our children safe is the work of every person, every day. It is our fiercest hope that this book can be a small contribution to the greatest of efforts.

Jennifer Stoltz's anguished cry following the loss of her child in the shooting at Sandy Hook Elementary still echoes years later: "If nothing changes out of this, then something is wrong" (Save the Children, 2013, p. 6). Tragically, not enough has changed in the area of school safety, and precious lives have been lost as a result. Something is indeed wrong, and it is up to us to change it.

# Resources

All of the resources mentioned in this book (along with many others) are available at www.eschoolsafety.org/resources. You can access these resources either by chapter (as they appear here) or by topic. Check the website often, as this section is updated and expanded frequently.

**Chapter 1—Where Did We Go Wrong?**
**The *States of Concern* report**—A yearly research report published by the Educator's School Safety Network that aggregates and analyzes data pertaining to threats and incidents of violence in U.S. schools.

**The *School-Based Bomb Incidents and Threats* report**—A yearly research report published by the Educator's School Safety Network that aggregates and analyzes data pertaining to school-based bomb threats and incidents.

**Letter from Secretary of Education John B. King Jr.**—An advisement to schools and universities regarding the role of school resource officers.

**SECURe Policy Rubric**—A Department of Justice rubric for states and local governments "looking to develop or revise statutes, regulations, and written agreements related to the appropriate incorporation of school-based law enforcement officers."

**Visitor Entry Screening training**—Education-based training for staff who will be using visitor entry systems or screening visitors to school buildings.

**Supplemental bibliography and links for other related resources**—Additional resources and materials related to topics discussed in this chapter.

## Chapter 2—Assessing for Vulnerabilities and Threats

*What Makes a Good Vulnerability Assessment?* **checklist**—The components of an effective vulnerability assessment, outlined in checklist form to assist in planning and evaluation.

*Tip Sheet for Intervention and Support*—Strategies and suggestions for creating and implementing appropriate supports and intervention related to the management of individuals of concern.

*Planning, Creating, Training, and Implementing a Threat Assessment Team*—A planning guide for getting started on threat assessment.

**Threat Assessment Management training**—Education-based training for threat assessment team members that combines content instruction, implementation strategies, and logistical concerns.

**Supplemental bibliography and links for other related resources**—Additional resources and materials related to topics discussed in this chapter.


## Chapter 3—Emergency Operations Plans

*Making Sense of the "Guide for Developing High-Quality School Emergency Operations Plans"*—A planning guide designed to assist educational leaders in creating, implementing, and evaluating a comprehensive, all-hazards emergency operations plan.

*Risk Matrix Worksheet*—A fillable PDF for use in planning, vulnerability assessments, and professional development.

**Incident Command Structure diagram**—A PDF of the incident command structure referenced in the chapter.

*What Does ICS Look Like in Schools?*—A graphical representation of the application of incident command to a typical school or district's organizational structure.

*Components of Comprehensive School and School District Emergency Management Plans*—A detailed description of the components of comprehensive, all-hazards emergency operation and management plans for use at building and district levels.

*Effective Supplemental Activities to Support Your School's EOP*—A collection of suggestions, samples, and links related to strategies and activities that support emergency planning.

**Supplemental bibliography and links to other related resources**—Additional and updated resources and materials related to topics discussed in this chapter.

### Chapter 4—Practicing and Living the Plan

*Empower Not Intimidate* **self-assessment**—Self-assessment to determine if the safety practices in schools empower or intimidate staff and students.

*A Common Vocabulary for Crisis Response in Schools*—A glossary of suggested crisis-management terms for use in developing a common vocabulary related to school safety.

**Supplemental bibliography and links for other related resources**—Additional resources and materials related to topics discussed in this chapter.

### Chapter 5—Bringing Lockdown Up-to-Date

**Post-incident debriefings and reports**—Reports from mass-casualty and school shooting incidents, including the shootings at Columbine High School, Virginia Tech, and Sandy Hook Elementary.

*Low-Cost, Effective Violence Prevention Strategies That Work*—A review of effective strategies for violence prevention in schools; includes related materials, links, and suggestions for implementation.

**Leveled-lockdown graphic**—A PDF graphic outlining leveled lockdown that can be used as a classroom sign or professional development handout.

*Is Our Response Effective?* **self-assessment**—A self-assessment checklist to look critically at the effectiveness of a school's active shooter and lockdown protocols.

**Lockdown Enhancements and Alternatives training**—Education-based training on lockdown enhancements and active shooter response.

**Supplemental bibliography and links for other related resources**—Additional resources and materials related to topics discussed in this chapter.

**Chapter 6—It's Not Just About Lockdown: Other Necessary Response Procedures**

**After-Hours Crisis Response training**—Education-based training on planning for and managing crisis response outside of traditional school hours.

*After-Hours Crisis Response Self-Assessment*—A self-assessment checklist to critically evaluate the effectiveness of a school's after-hours crisis response capabilities.

*An After-Hours Crisis Response Planning Guide for Schools*—A planning guide designed for educational leaders to assist in creating, implementing, and evaluating effective crisis response procedures outside of traditional school hours.

The *School-Based Bomb Incidents and Threats* report—An annual research report published by the Educator's School Safety Network that aggregates and analyzes data pertaining to school-based bomb threats and incidents.

**School-Based Bomb Incident Management training**—Education-based training on planning for and responding to bomb incidents, including threats, suspicious items, and detonations.

**Supplemental bibliography and links for other related resources**— Additional resources and materials related to topics discussed in this chapter.

**Chapter 7—What to Do After the Initial Response**

**Emergency Communication Templates**—Samples and tips for creating emergency communication templates.

*Implementing Family Emergency Plans with School Staff Members*—A checklist with suggestions for ensuring that all staff members have active, updated family emergency plans.

**Family Emergency Plan Templates**—Samples and templates for creating family emergency plans.

**Supplemental bibliography and links for other related resources**— Additional resources and materials related to topics discussed in this chapter.

## Chapter 8—Recovering, Reflecting, and Learning

*A Continuity of Operations Planning Guide for Schools*—A planning guide designed for educational leaders to assist in creating, implementing, and evaluating a continuity of operations plan.

*Standard Reunification Method Planning Guide*—A link to download-able materials for parent reunification from the "I Love U Guys" Foundation.

**Parent Reunification training**—Education-based training on the facility, staffing, accountability, and logistical concerns involved in planning and implementing parent reunification.

**The PREPaRE Model**—Information on the National Association of School Psychologists' PREPaRE Model for crisis intervention and recovery.

**Supplemental bibliography and links for other related resources**—Additional resources and materials related to topics discussed in this chapter.

# References

American Association of School Administrators. (2010, May 18). *School budgets 101.* Available: https://www.aasa.org/uploadedFiles/Policy_and_Advocacy/files/ SchoolBudgetBriefFINAL.pdf

Blair, J. P., Martaindale, M. H., & Nichols, T. (2014, January). Active shooter events from 2000 to 2012. *FBI Law Enforcement Bulletin.* Available: https://leb.fbi. gov/2014/january/active-shooter-events-from-2000-to-2012

Blair, J. P., & Schweit, K. W. (2014). *A study of active shooter incidents, 2000–2013.* Washington, DC: Texas State University and Federal Bureau of Investigation, U.S. Department of Justice. Available: https://www.fbi.gov/file-repository/ active-shooter-study-2000-2013-1.pdf

Brock, S., Nickerson, A., Louvar Reeves, M., Conolly, C., Jimerson, S., Pesce, R., & Lazzaro, B. (2016). *School crisis prevention and intervention: The PREPaRE model* (2nd ed.). Bethesda, MD: National Association of School Psychologists.

Brock, S. E., Nickerson, A. B., Reeves, M. A., Jimerson, S. R., Lieberman, R. A., & Feinberg, T. A. (2009). *School crisis prevention and intervention.* Bethesda, MD: National Association of School Psychologists.

Brymer, M., Jacobs, A., Layne, C., Pynoos, R., Ruzek, J., Steinberg, A., et al. (2006). *Psychological first aid: Field operations guide* (2nd ed.). Rockville, MD: National Child Traumatic Stress Network and National Center for PTSD.

Bureau of Alcohol, Tobacco, Firearms and Explosives. (2003). *Bomb threat response: An interactive planning tool for schools* [CD-ROM]. Washington, DC: Bureau of Alcohol, Tobacco, Firearms and Explosives, U.S. Department of the Treasury, and the Safe and Drug-Free Schools Program, U.S. Department of Education.

Cowan, D., & Kuenster, J. (1996). *To sleep with the angels: The story of a fire.* Chicago: Ivan R. Dee.

Dorn, M. (2015, January). Active shooter training under fire again. *School Safety Monthly,* 4–6. Retrieved from http://safehavensinternational.org/wp-content/ uploads/School_Safety_Monthly-Jan_2015-Safe_Havens_Intl.pdf

Dorn, M. (2015, May 13). Lawsuit filed by school employee injured in ALICE training [blog post]. Available: http://safehavensinternational.org/lawsuit-filed-school-employee-injured-alice-training/

Dorn, M., & Dorn, C. (2005). *Innocent targets: When terrorism comes to school.* Macon, GA: Safe Havens International.

Energetic Materials Research and Testing Center. (2010, November). *Incident response to terrorist bombings* (National Domestic Preparedness Consortium Publication No. PER 230-1). Socorro, NM: Author.

Federal Emergency Management Agency (FEMA). (n.d.). *Are you ready? An in-depth guide to citizen preparedness.* Washington, DC: Author.

Federal Emergency Management Agency (FEMA). (n.d.). *Multihazard emergency planning for schools site index.* Available: https://training.fema.gov/programs/emischool/el361toolkit/siteindex.htm#item4

Federal Emergency Management Agency (FEMA). (2010, November). *Developing and maintaining emergency operations plans* (CPG 101, Version 2.0). Washington, DC: Government Printing Office. Available: https://www.fema.gov/media-library-data/20130726-1828-25045-0014/cpg_101_comprehensive_preparedness_guide_developing_and_maintaining_emergency_operations_plans_2010.pdf

Federal Emergency Management Agency (FEMA). (2011, March). *Sample school emergency operations plan E/L361 and G364: Multihazard emergency planning for schools.* Washington, DC: Author.

Federal Emergency Management Agency (FEMA). (2016, February 12). *Preparedness cycle.* Available: https://www.fema.gov/media-library/assets/images/114295

Goodrum, S., & Woodward, W. (2016, January). *Report on the Arapahoe High School shooting: Lessons learned on information sharing, threat assessment, and systems integrity.* Boulder, CO: University of Colorado Boulder.

Governors Columbine Review Commission. (2001). *The report of Governor Bill Owens' Columbine Review Commission.* Denver, CO: Author.

Green, E. (2017, August 8). The JCC bomb-threat suspect had a client. *The Atlantic.* Available: https://www.theatlantic.com/politics/archive/2017/08/the-jcc-bomb-threat-maker-had-a-buyer/536193/

Jones, J. M. (Ed.). (2017, August 17). Parental fear about school safety back to pre-Newtown level. Available: http://news.gallup.com/poll/216308/parental-fear-school-safety-back-pre-newtown-level.aspx

Kentucky Center for School Safety. (2016). *Emergency management resource guides.* Richmond, KY: Author. Available: http://www.kycss.org/clear/emgpage.php

Keyes, J.-M. (2011). *Standard reunification method: A practical method to unite students with parents after an evacuation or crisis.* Bailey, CO: "I Love U Guys" Foundation. Available: http://iloveuguys.org/srm/Standard%20Reunification%20Method.pdf

Klinger, A. L., & Klinger, A. L. (2016). *Bomb incidents in schools: An analysis of the 2015–2016 school year.* Genoa, OH: Educator's School Safety Network.

Klinger, A. L., & Klinger, A. L. (2017). *States of concern: An analysis of U.S. states with high rates of school-based violent threats and incidents.* Genoa, OH: Educator's School Safety Network.

Maslow, A. H. (1943). A theory of human motivation. *Psychological Review, 50*(4): 370–396.

McFarland, J., Hussar, B., de Brey, C., Snyder, T., Wang, X., Wilkinson-Flicker, S., et al. (2017). *The condition of education 2017* (NCES 2017- 144). Washington, DC: U.S. Department of Education, National Center for Education Statistics. Available: https://nces.ed.gov/pubsearch/pubsinfo.asp?pubid=2017144

McGurk, H., & Hurry, J. (1995). *Project Charlie: An evaluation of a life skills drug education programme for primary students.* London: Drugs Prevention Initiative.

National Institute of Mental Health (NIMH). (2001). *Mental health and mass violence: Evidence-based early psychological intervention for victims/survivors of mass violence. A workshop to reach consensus on best practices.* Washington, DC: Author.

New York Police Department Counterterrorism Bureau. (2011, January 20). *Active shooter: Recommendations and analysis for risk mitigation.* New York: Author.

New York Police Department Counterterrorism Bureau. (2012). *Active shooter: Recommendations and analysis for risk mitigation, 2012 edition.* New York: Author. Available: http://www.nyc.gov/html/nypd/downloads/pdf/counterterrorism/ActiveShooter2012Edition.pdf

Newman, G. R. (2011, August). *Bomb threats in schools* (Publication No. 32). Albany, NY: Center for Problem-Oriented Policing.

Office of Emergency Communications. (2010, June). *Plain language frequently asked questions (FAQs).* Washington, DC: Department of Homeland Security.

Prevention Institute. (n.d.). *Violence and learning* [Fact sheet]. Oakland, CA: Author. Available: https://www.preventioninstitute.org/sites/default/files/publications/Fact%20Sheet%20Links%20Between%20Violence%20and%20Learning.pdf

Save the Children. (2013). *Unaccounted for: A national report card on protecting children in disasters.* Washington, DC: Author.

Schlecty, P. (2005). *Creating great schools: Six critical systems at the heart of educational innovation.* San Francisco: Jossey-Bass.

Sedensky, S. J. (2013). *Report of the state's attorney for the judicial district of Danbury on the shootings at Sandy Hook Elementary School and 36 Yogananda Street, Newtown, Connecticut on December 14, 2012*. Danbury, CT: Office of the State's Attorney.

Sherwood, B. (2009). *The survivors club: The secrets and science that could save your life*. New York: Grand Central Publishing.

Soergel, A. (2017, September 8). 5 things to know about the economy this week. *U.S. News and World Report*. Available: https://www.usnews.com/news/economy/slideshows/trump-talks-taxes-equifax-breached-and-5-things-to-know-about-the-economy

Stephens, R. D. (n.d.). Director's message. National School Safety Center [Website]. Available: http://www.schoolsafety.us/about-us/director-s-message

U.S. Department of Education. (2016). Obama administration releases resources for schools and college to ensure appropriate use of school resource officers and campus police [Press release]. Washington, DC: Author. Available: https://www.ed.gov/news/press-releases/obama-administration-releases-resources-schools-colleges-ensure-appropriate-use-school-resource-officers-and-campus-police

U.S. Department of Education, Office of Elementary and Secondary Education [OESE], Office of Safe and Healthy Students [OSHS]. (2013). *Guide for developing high-quality school emergency operations plans*. Washington, DC: Authors.

U.S. Department of Education & U.S. Department of Justice. (2016). *Safe school-based enforcement through collaboration, understanding, and respect: SECURe state and local policy rubric*. Washington, DC: Author.

U.S. Department of Homeland Security. (2017, September). Plan and prepare for disasters [Web page]. Available: https://www.dhs.gov/topic/plan-and-prepare-disasters

Virginia Tech Review Panel. (2007, April 16). *Mass shootings at Virginia Tech*. Available: http://cdm16064.contentdm.oclc.org/cdm/ref/collection/p266901coll4/id/904

Vossekuil, B., Fein, R., Reddy, M., Borum, R., & Modzeleski, W. (2002). *The final report and findings of the Safe School Initiative: Implications for the prevention of school attacks in the United States*. Washington, DC: U.S. Secret Service and U.S. Department of Education.

Zhang, A., Musu-Gillette, L., & Oudekerk, B. A. (2016). *Indicators of school crime and safety: 2015* (NCES 2016-079/NCJ 249758). Washington, DC: National Center for Education Statistics, U.S. Department of Education; and Bureau of Justice Statistics, Office of Justice Programs, U.S. Department of Justice.

# Index

The letter *f* following a page number denotes a figure.

# About the Authors

  **Amy Klinger,** EdD, and **Amanda Klinger,** Esq., are nationally recognized experts on school safety and crisis management. They are cofounders of the Educator's School Safety Network, which provides training, resources, and technical assistance to schools throughout the United States and Canada (www.eschoolsafety.org).

In addition to direct training with educators and law enforcement officers, Amy and Amanda are frequent presenters at regional, state, national, and international conferences on school safety and security. They conduct ongoing research on threats and incidents of violence in schools and frequently appear on or are interviewed by national media outlets on topics related to violence prevention, crisis response, and school safety.

Amy has more than 28 years of experience in public education as a teacher, an elementary and secondary principal, and a central office administrator. She is an associate professor of educational leadership and program director at Ashland University in Ashland, Ohio. Amanda has a law degree from Akron University School of Law in Akron, Ohio, and previously practiced law in North Carolina, where she represented criminal defendants and worked in the juvenile justice system.

# Related ASCD Resources

At the time of publication, the following resources were available (ASCD stock numbers in parentheses).

*Educational Leadership:* Mental Health in Schools (December 2017/January 2018) (#118066)

*Educational Leadership:* Disrupting Inequity (November 2016) (#117039)

*Educational Leadership:* Emotionally Healthy Kids (October 2015) (#116029)

*Fostering Resilient Learners: Strategies for Creating a Trauma-Sensitive Classroom* (#116014)

*Keeping the Whole Child Healthy and Safe: Reflections on Best Practices in Learning, Teaching, and Leadership* (#110130E4)

*Teaching to Strengths: Supporting Students Living with Trauma, Violence, and Chronic Stress* (#117035)

For up-to-date information about ASCD resources, go to www.ascd.org. You can search the complete archives of *Educational Leadership* at www.ascd.org/el.

**ASCD myTeachSource®**
Download resources from a professional learning platform with hundreds of research-based best practices and tools for your classroom at http://myteachsource.ascd.org/

For more information, send an e-mail to member@ascd.org; call 1-800-933-2723 or 703-578-9600; send a fax to 703-575-5400; or write to Information Services, ASCD, 1703 N. Beauregard St., Alexandria, VA 22311-1714 USA.

# WHOLE CHILD
# **TENETS**

## ① **HEALTHY**
Each student enters school healthy and learns about and practices a healthy lifestyle.

## ② **SAFE**
Each student learns in an environment that is physically and emotionally safe for students and adults.

## ③ **ENGAGED**
Each student is actively engaged in learning and is connected to the school and broader community.

## ④ **SUPPORTED**
Each student has access to personalized learning and is supported by qualified, caring adults.

## ⑤ **CHALLENGED**
Each student is challenged academically and prepared for success in college or further study and for employment and participation in a global environment.

The ASCD Whole Child approach is an effort to transition from a focus on narrowly defined academic achievement to one that promotes the long-term development and success of all children. Through this approach, ASCD supports educators, families, community members, and policymakers as they move from a vision about educating the whole child to sustainable, collaborative actions.

*Keeping Students Safe Every Day* relates to the **safety** tenet.
*For more about the ASCD Whole Child approach, visit*
**www.ascd.org/wholechild.**